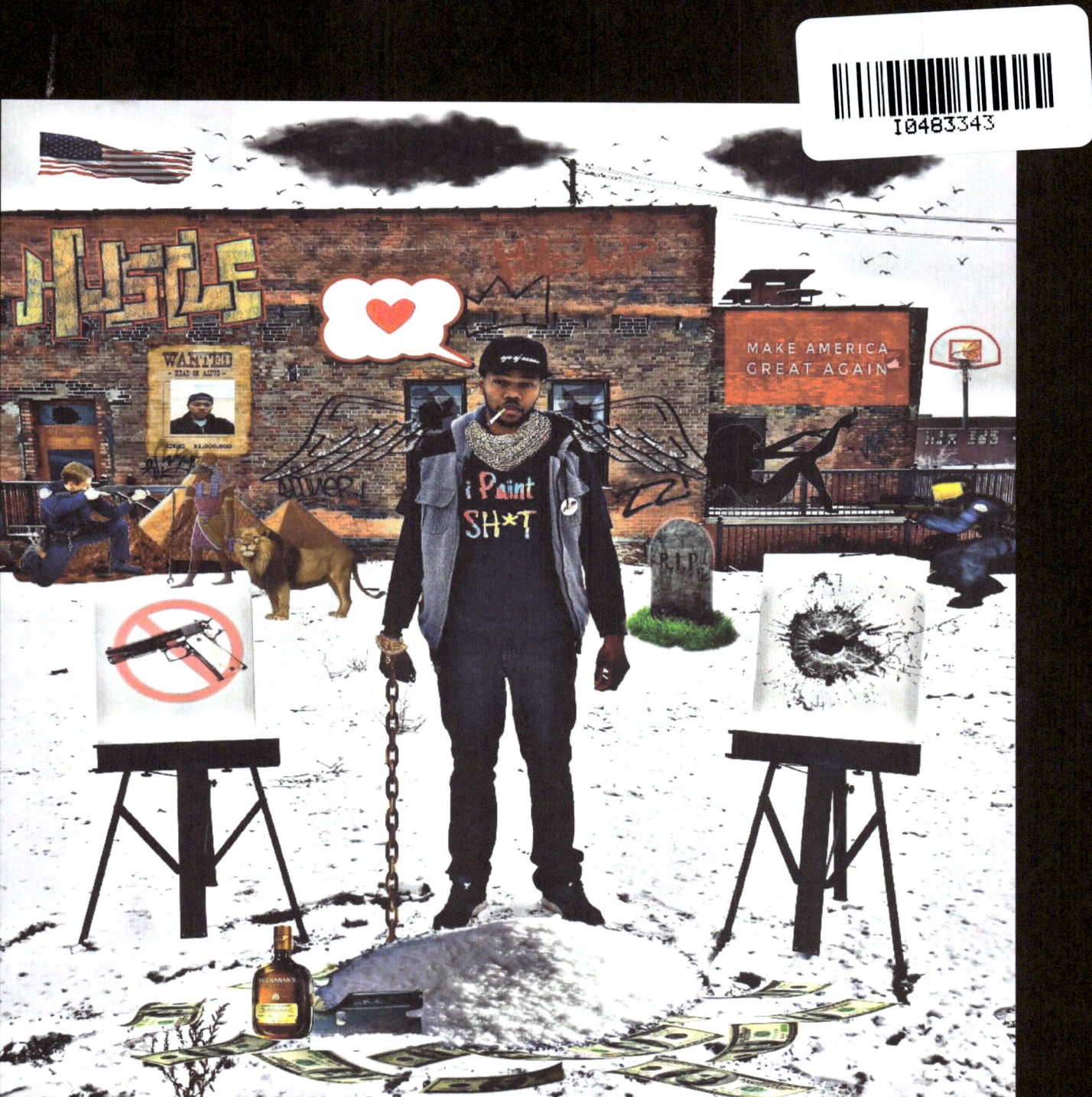

Poetry, Paintings & **Protest**

Ivan Azaan Tarver

Edited by Markesha Tarver

I dedicate this book to my mom, wife and everybody that has supported my art throughout the years. Without your love and support this book wouldn't be possible. I love you and I hope I make you proud.

Introduction

    I began writing this book for myself. My poetry is a form of therapy for me. It's crazy, because prior to this, I hadn't written in almost 10 years due to writer's block. One day I just couldn't write anymore so I chose to give up. In 2017, I was battling depression and I wanted to find a way to channel my thoughts, so I started writing. Just like that, I started writing again almost every day.

    I was inspired to write the poems and paint the pictures in this book by many different things. There is so much going on in the world. We are all fighting for change. I feel that we are at a critical point in history today. With everything that's going on, we have the opportunity to make a difference. Creating this book is my way of doing my part to help. We have been fighting for equality and fair treatment since the beginning of time. Many people are taking a stand and fighting for what they believe in today. I'm inspired to be a part of the fight for change. The poems and paintings included in this book are very personal. It is my hope that this book provides inspiration. I hope my struggles and my story can help inspire the next person.

Freedom of Speech Mural

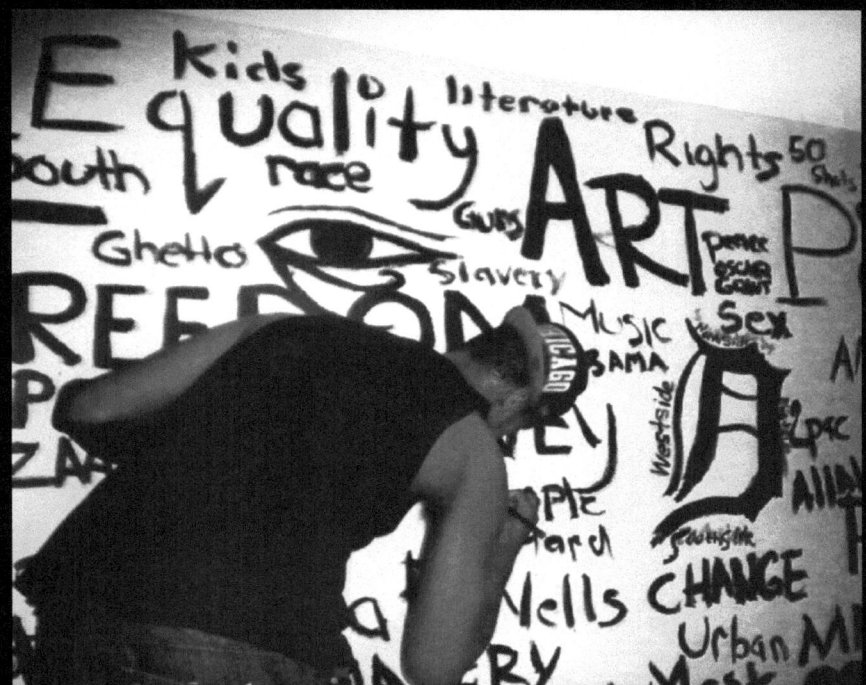

Untitled (My first painting)

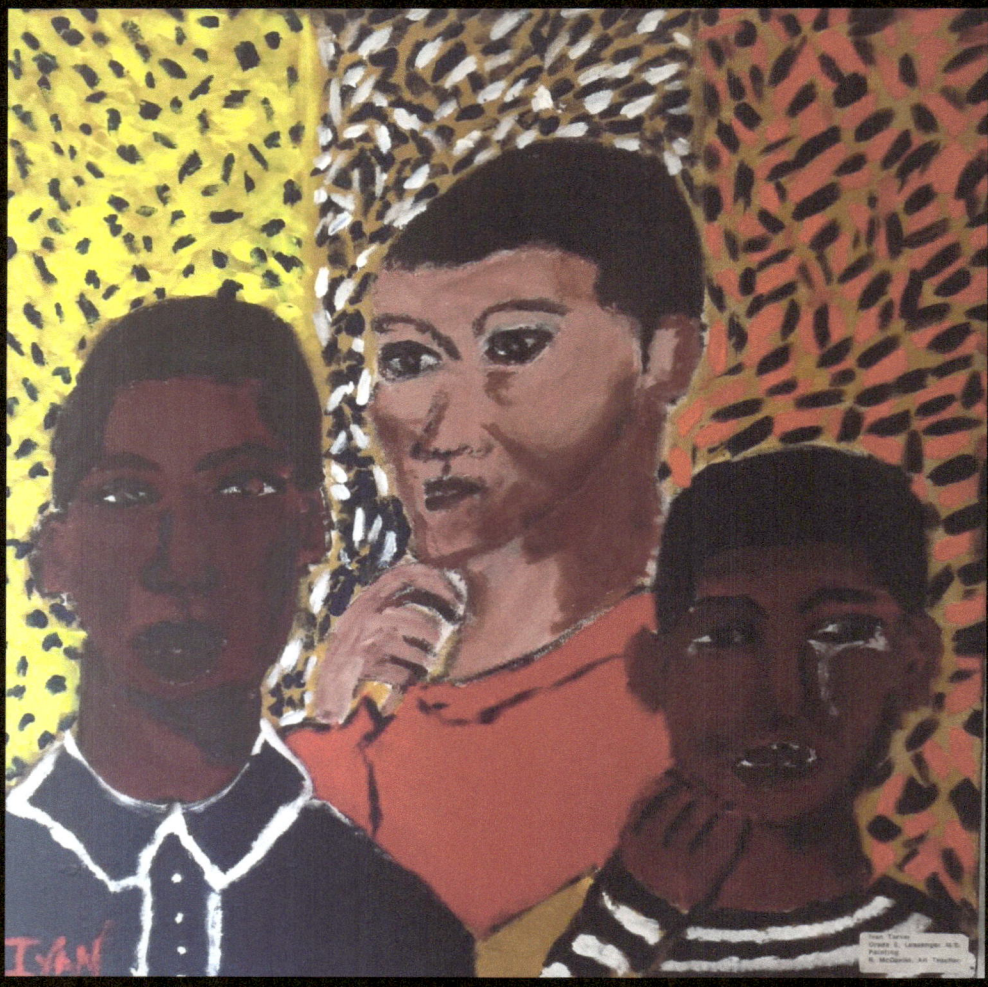

Acrylic painting on canvas.

Detroit, Michigan 1999.

Self-Portrait

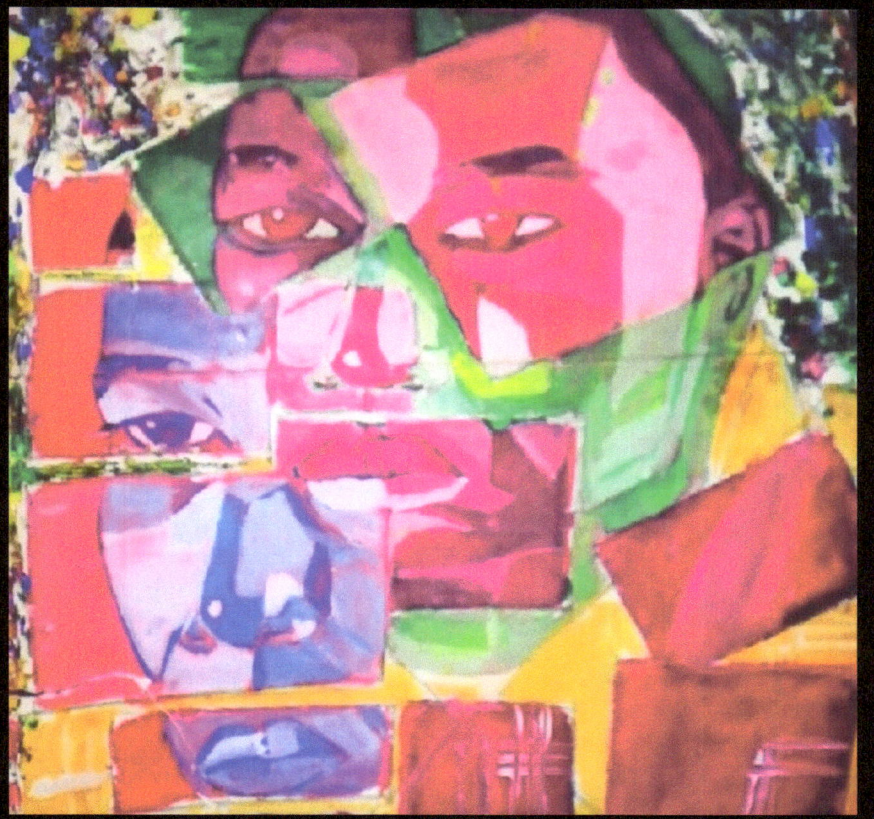

Acrylic painting on canvas.

Detroit, Michigan 2002.

A Father

Nothing like hearing the baritone voice

of the man you look up to.

The verbal vibrations that come out his mouth

travel through the walls and the vents.

As the bass guitar plays,

I know trouble is near.

Guilt becomes apparent,

when the instrumental no longer plays.

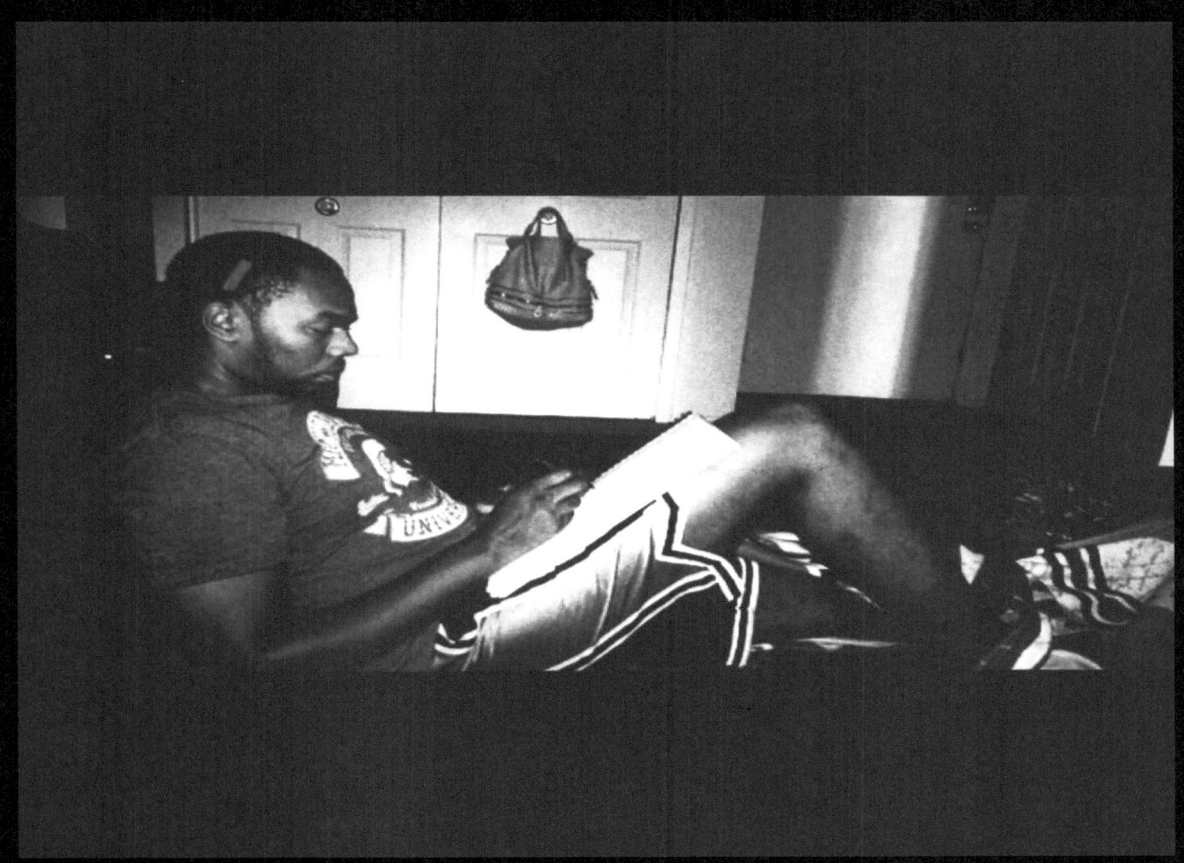

Southfield, Michigan 2015.

Born 2 Fail

I was configured to be a robot

described as a savage beast

born to be a surrogate,

placed on segregated reservations

where I was supposed to be a worker

to build a world distant from humanity.

I was never human, you see

never granted immunity from a broken community.

I was left abandoned and abused like Oscar Grant and Derrion Albert.

Society looked me in my eyes

and told me I was destined to fail.

Showed me the scriptures that were written in the bible

as they tattooed the mark of the beast on my forehead.

So, you see

I was born sick

Born with the same shit

that my father had

his father had

and his father had.

I'm a product of a bunch of mixed up chromosomes.

My pops left his DNA

and let my mother give birth alone.

To a victim of a lost generation

who search for donors

on corners

and in the office of coroners.

Trying to make sense of this eternal coma

that someday we hope to wake up from

and we do wake up

we will probably wake up numb,

with a fully loaded gun.

Dripping hollow tips

from these blinded eyes

that blow up every time

headlines run across eyes.

Saying 7-year-old boy

got shot on his way to school,

this is what we live through.

Killing each other

over the same broken promises

And signing promissory notes

For loans we can't pay.

But we will risk it all for the green paper

with red spots and dead presidents on it.

This is all we know.

Ain't no therapist we can afford,

so, we go to our street fam for the intervention

but the diagnosis

remains the same.

We are all young men that need help.

We need mentors

to navigate us through this thing called manhood

And explain this thing that hangs in between our thighs

And its proper usage.

Because lately I've been using it to hurt women.

Not from pleasure

but from the strokes of pain that I give them as I lay on top of them.

And when I cum,

I secrete confessions of my love that hid behind my erection.

You know like

"I love you baby,

but I gotta go

because we are getting too close

and the pressure forces me to let go

I know

I need help"

Mentally and emotionally.

I wasn't built for relationships

I was built for slavery institutions

because historically that has been the solution for people

Like me.

Especially when you're trained to bang like Tookie and slang like Lucas

ain't no love out there.

Especially for shorty that's trying to be a thug.

You know it's messed up when you feel uncomfortable giving your own mama a hug.

That's what I call dysfunctional love.

But that's what it's about

Those 4 letters.

A lot of men are good actors

potential Denzel's and Will Smith's

but if you look behind the mask we wear

You will find love

The love of a man.

Black Boy

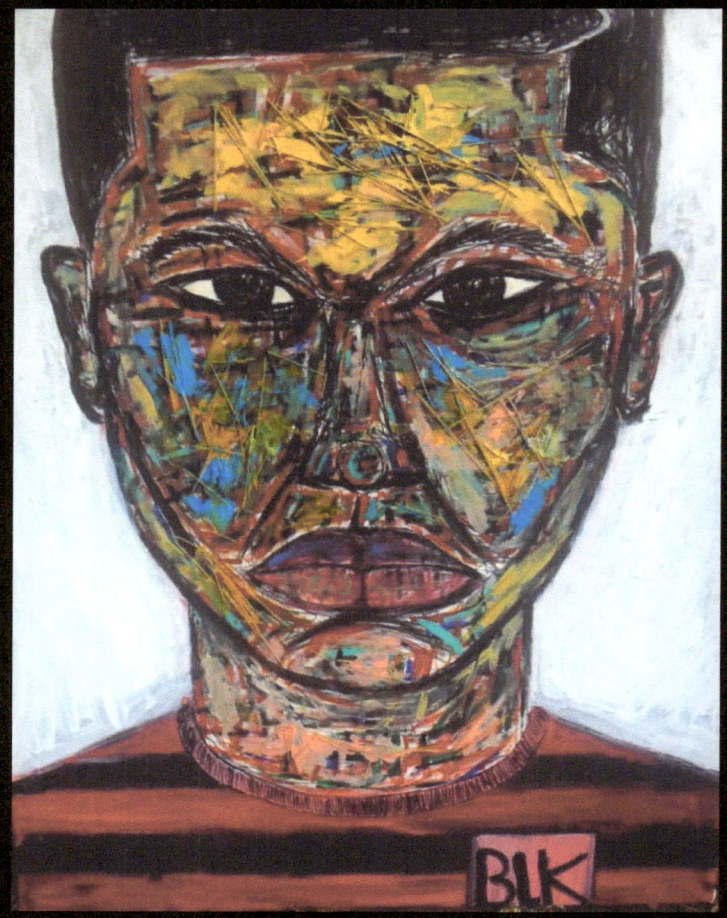

Mixed Media painting on canvas. 36 in x 48 in.

Southfield, Michigan 2015.

Watoto

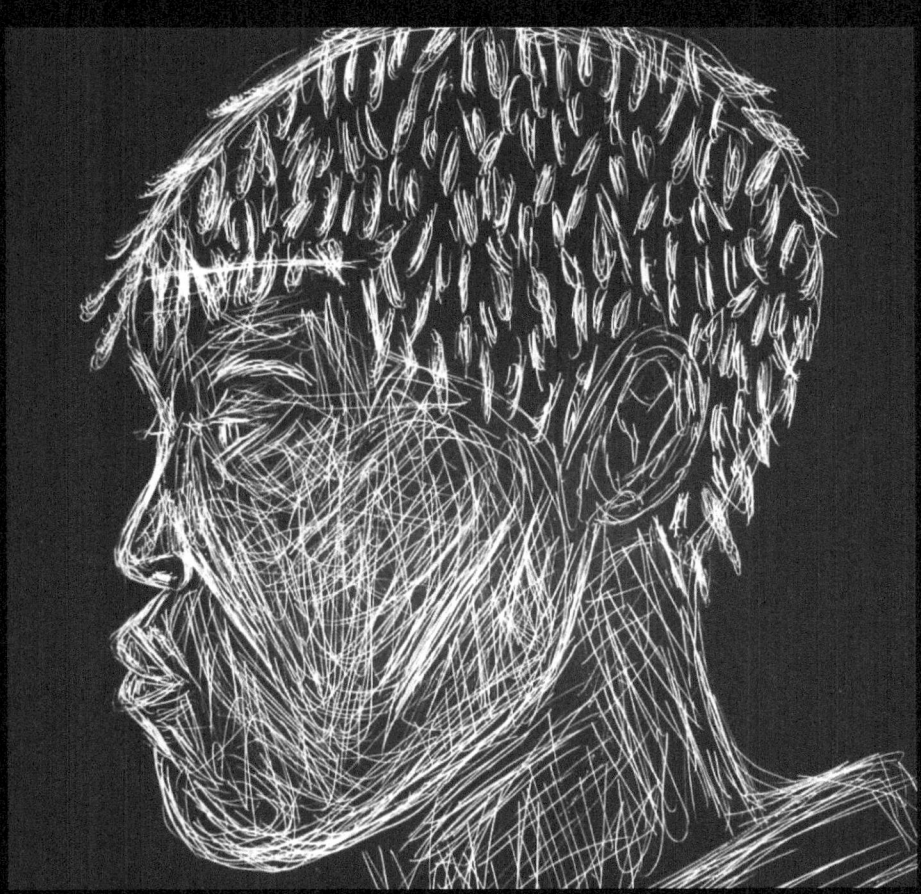

Scratchboard. 12 in x 16 in.

Detroit, Michigan 2015.

Dedicated to The Future

Where I'm from

the kids were born in caskets.

Born with an ending in search of a beginning

stuck in the middle

between trying to survive and sinning.

Looking for how-to-guides and self-help books

in an unhealthy place.

Trying to find optimistic boulevard

but the world left you no trace.

No clear path

so innocent souls

settle for roles

taught by corrupted models

who submerged their thoughts in liquor bottles

and spit scriptures on corners and in alleys

talkin' bout walkin' through valleys

and not fearing death.

This is the life through

the eyes of these kids.

No more fantasy stories

like Sesame Street or The Wiz.

Because little boys and girls

become more amused with the hustlers outside and the fancy rides

preoccupied with the reasons behind

why dreams and reality collide.

The old folks say prayer is the only way

they say you must enter the church to witness the Lord's work.

A sanctified place

where the preachers are preaching

trying to reach the youth

by teaching what they call the truth.

But their words only travel so far

because It's hard to spit knowledge

when you got lil shorties on the block

sayin' they atheists

because they hate this shit

livin' below the poverty line.

thinkin' one day maybe

I can climb to the middle

so I can be in a class

where the books aren't missing pages

and the teachers can finish the lesson plan

they planned

before the day ends.

No lights

no food in the ghetto.

Just gun shots

and constant screams

In between the drug dealers and the senseless fiends.

The mornings become dark

The sun is blocked by the clouds

another mother mourns the loss of her child

another innocent bystander standing in the wrong place

another A student

another good kid

on a ride to prosperity and happiness.

Now they're still on that same ride

just on a different route

the route that many young souls take.

Like on the streets of Chicago

where the government quick to street sweep and talk about Olympic bids

But what about these kids.

Kids are the future.

The brick holders of architecture

that have not yet been finished or started.

All they need is the opportunity to be somebody their father wasn't

and somebody their mother tried to be.

All they need is the opportunity

To believe.

OBAMA FOREVER

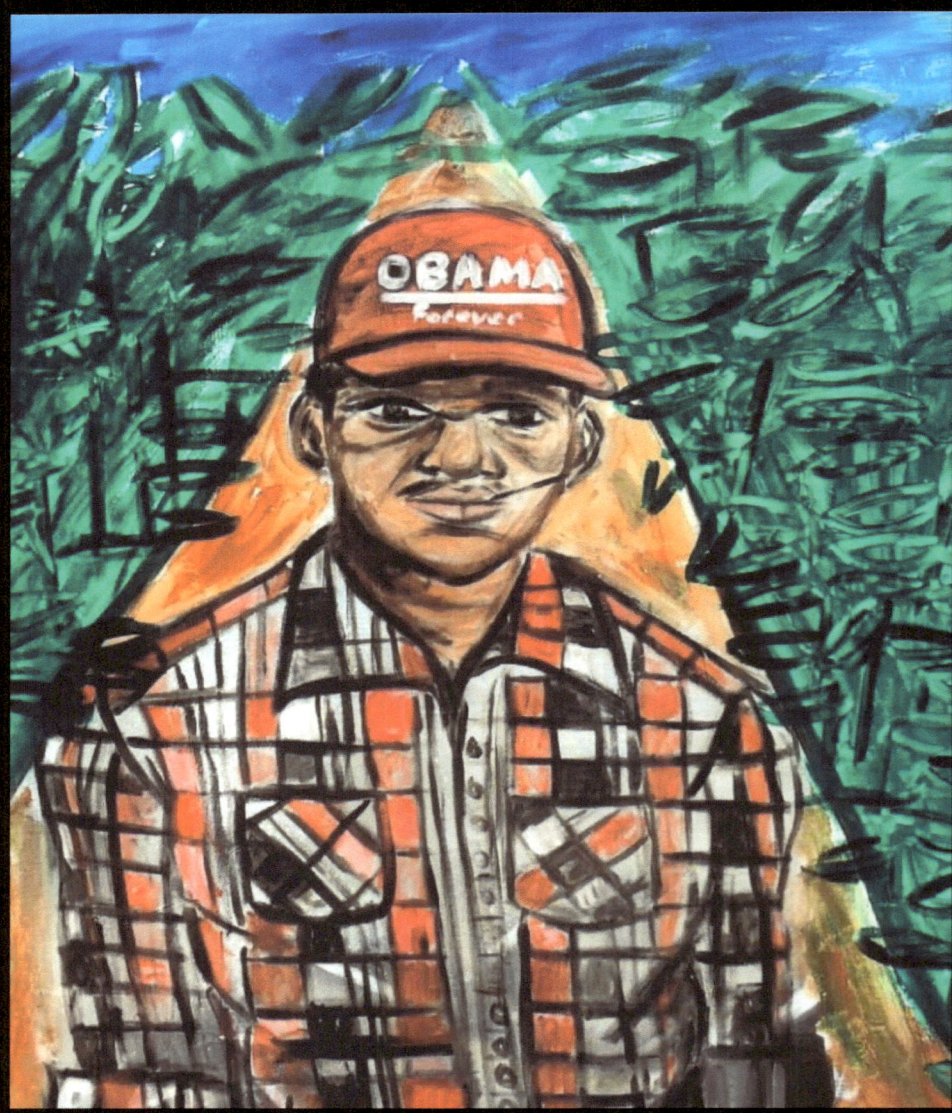

Acrylic painting on canvas. 36 in X 48 in.

Redford, Michigan 2017.

Bring Barack Back

Bring number 44 back

his cool swag

his stylish wife

those beautiful kids

and even Bo.

We are living in terrible times.

Trumped.

Stuck in a divided country.

Red or Blue.

This is a reality show

so surreal

I can't wait to wake up.

I don't feel safe.

Take me back to 2008.

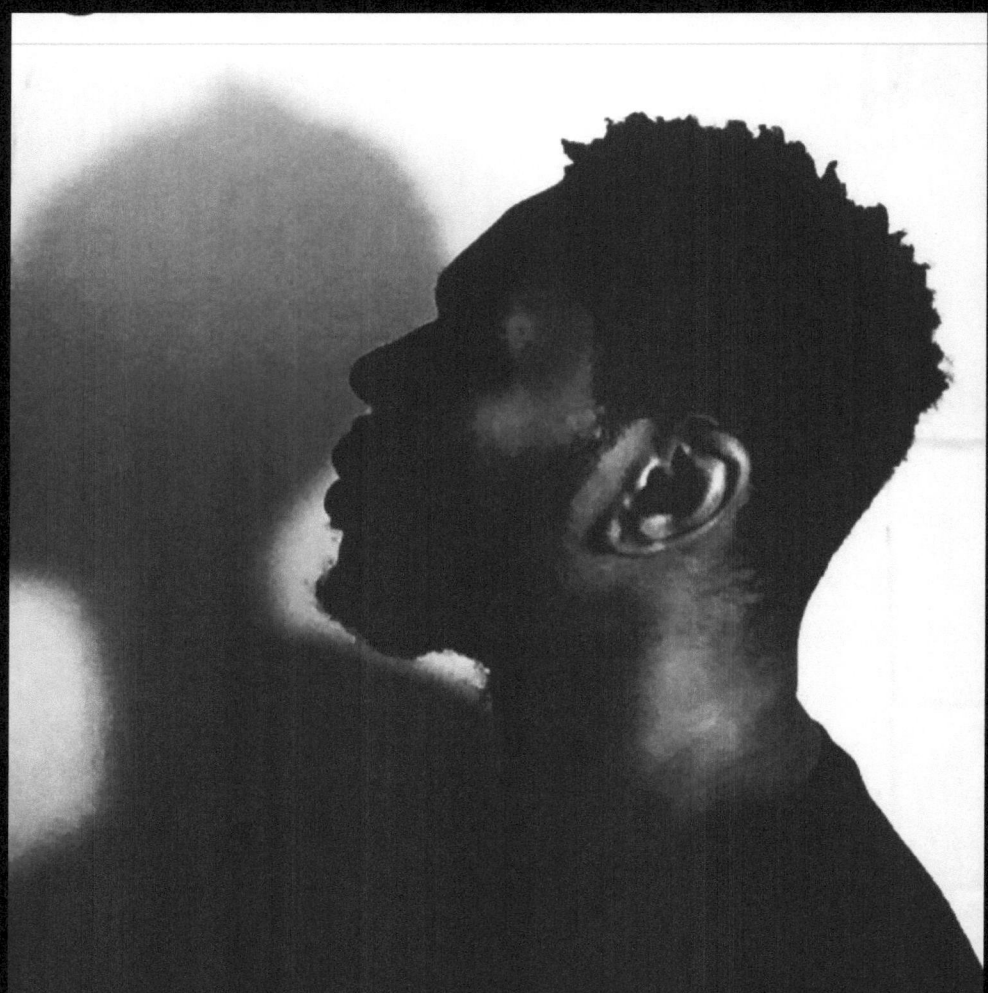

Redford, Michigan 2017

Changed Man

I was

searching for better

striving for change

walking through sewers and manure

just to come out newer.

Getting dirty

just to be worthy.

All the growing pains

helped me maintain.

The road to becoming

has been difficult.

But it

made me stronger.

I remember

lying face down in that parking lot

God made days a little bit longer

instead of being hit with a taser

I could've been shot.

Another Black Male

stupid me

taking shots of moonshine

staring at the moon light

searching for Christ.

Blurry and distorted

My world was upside down.

I was

homeless

feeling less

subtracted from home

nothing really added value to my life.

Mistake after mistake

asking questions

like

Is this right

and God do you hate me?

I just don't understand these pages

the words are smeared

hopefully this chapter doesn't end

with me suffering another year.

Me and my brother not talking.

This depression gettin' the best of me.

She says I love you

but I don't hear her.

Because the shouting and finger pointing

got me questioning the stranger I see in the mirror

he just doesn't look familiar.

They say

This stress will kill ya

leave you bodied

have you drinking like it's a hobby.

I know.

Life is so complex

it's so hard to concentrate.

Maybe I should become a Buddhist and go meditate

or read the bible and find faith.

The homies say I should roll up

Levitate

Touch the sky

Converse with the angels.

Because those demons will hang you

Leave your body battered and blue

your family can't recognize you.

Unrecognizable

people can't wait to criticize you

talk about the bad

judge you by your past

like change ain't gon come

Like Barack or Sam said.

I'm blessed to be here

because a lot of the homies are dead.

Chasing dreams and fast money

ever since a baby

we were taught it's all about the Cash Money.

I got to stay focused

even though my visions

resemble a kaleidoscope

I still gotta have hope

For a brighter future.

Tomorrows might bring sorrow

but they also bring opportunity

And a fresh start

All I gotta do is

Follow my heart.

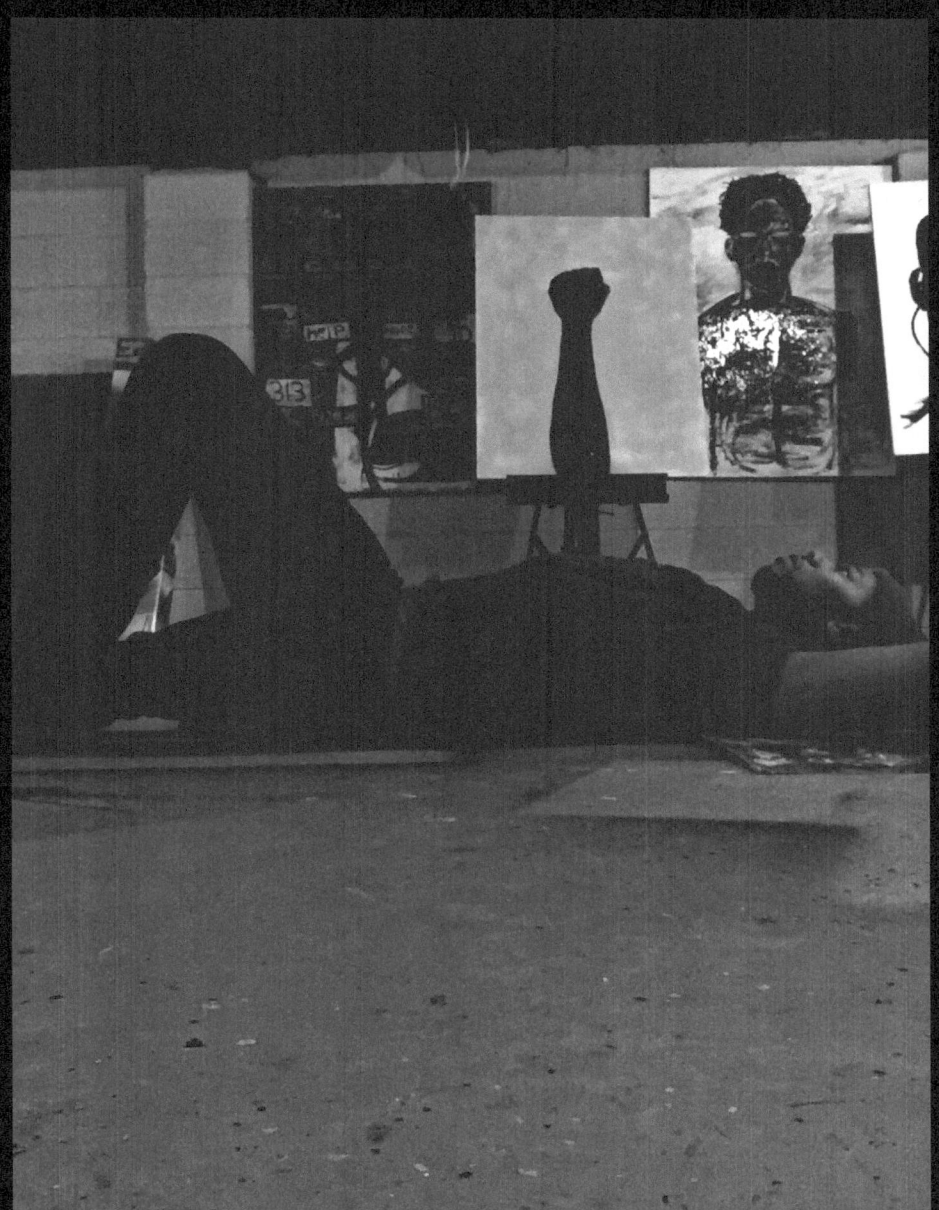

Redford, Michigan 2017

Ashamed

Why should I be ashamed?

I am human

just like YOU.

I smile and frown

just like YOU.

I cry at funerals

just like YOU.

No.

I am not perfect

but perfection is not what I'm looking for,

I'm looking for understanding

In fact

I'm demanding Freedom

because these chains are too tight

I'm starting to the feel numbness in my hand

thinking...

Was this part of the plan?

I know they say the last shall be first

but listen...

I'm so tired of getting hurt

and the minute you think it can't get worse

another line of full cars

and a Black boy laying in a hearse.

We are fighting for equality

In an unequal space.

No room to move

so, we must fight

to find our way out.

With every bone

every limb

we sing hymns

and work songs

to communicate.

Back in the day

all we had was faith

even though we were facing hate.

This was our mutual understanding.

My ancestors bled for me

their struggle led me to see

that this little light of mine

can still can shine

even in the darkest tunnels.

Even though hard times can leave you disoriented

we still push forward

toward bright lights and clear futures,

We come from greatness.

My ancestors

Use to pray at the top of pyramids

were architects and chemists

Products of Kemet.

Trust me

I am no different

we are different

but our differences

connect us.

History displaced our thoughts

Left humanity

For dead.

Said we were slaves

because that's what the bible said

false interpretations

kept us racing

divided the races

I guess that's why today

we are still talking about racism.

Psychological warfare.

Greed has stunted the growth of young seeds

that refuse to grow

maybe because they don't know

or maybe they weren't told

They were beautiful or great.

The stars are yours

all you have to do is dream.

Trust I am no different

I am You

And you are me.

Where I'm From

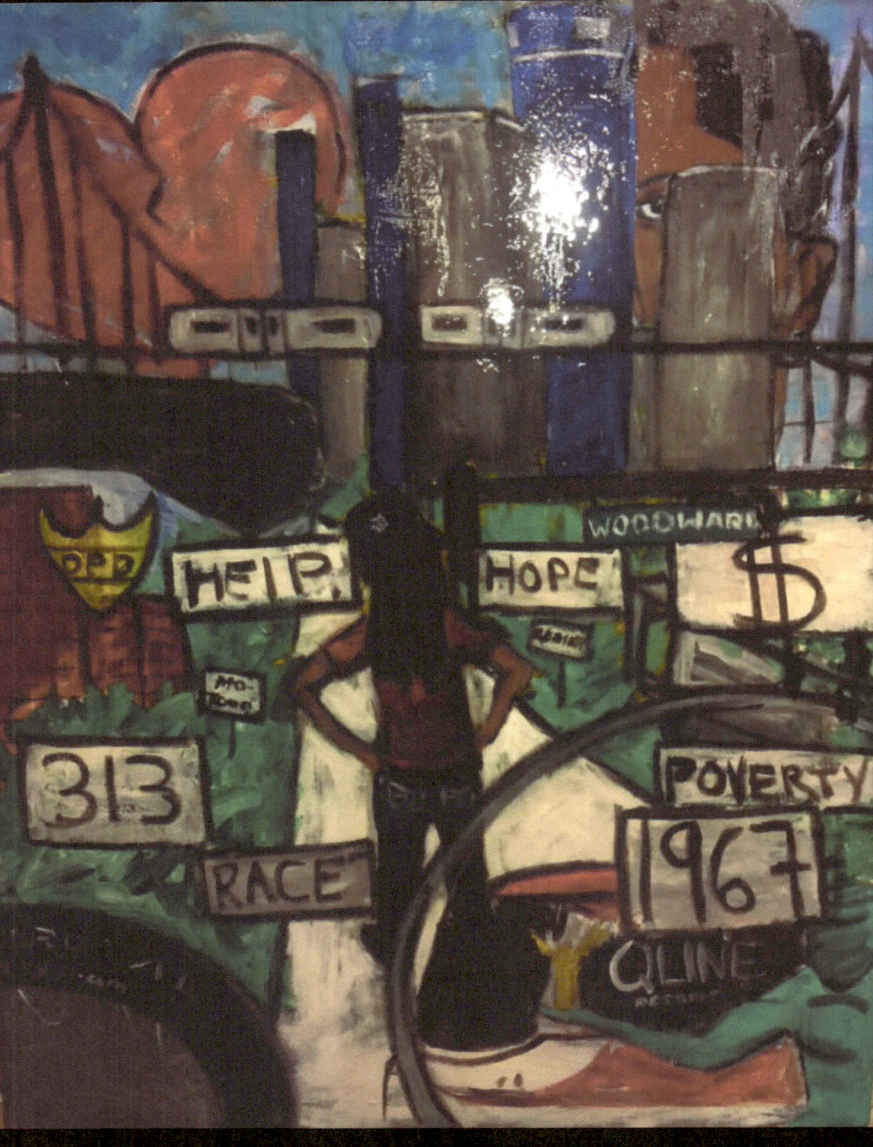

Acrylic painting on canvas. 36 in x 48 in.

Detroit, Michigan 2017

Detroit Mentality

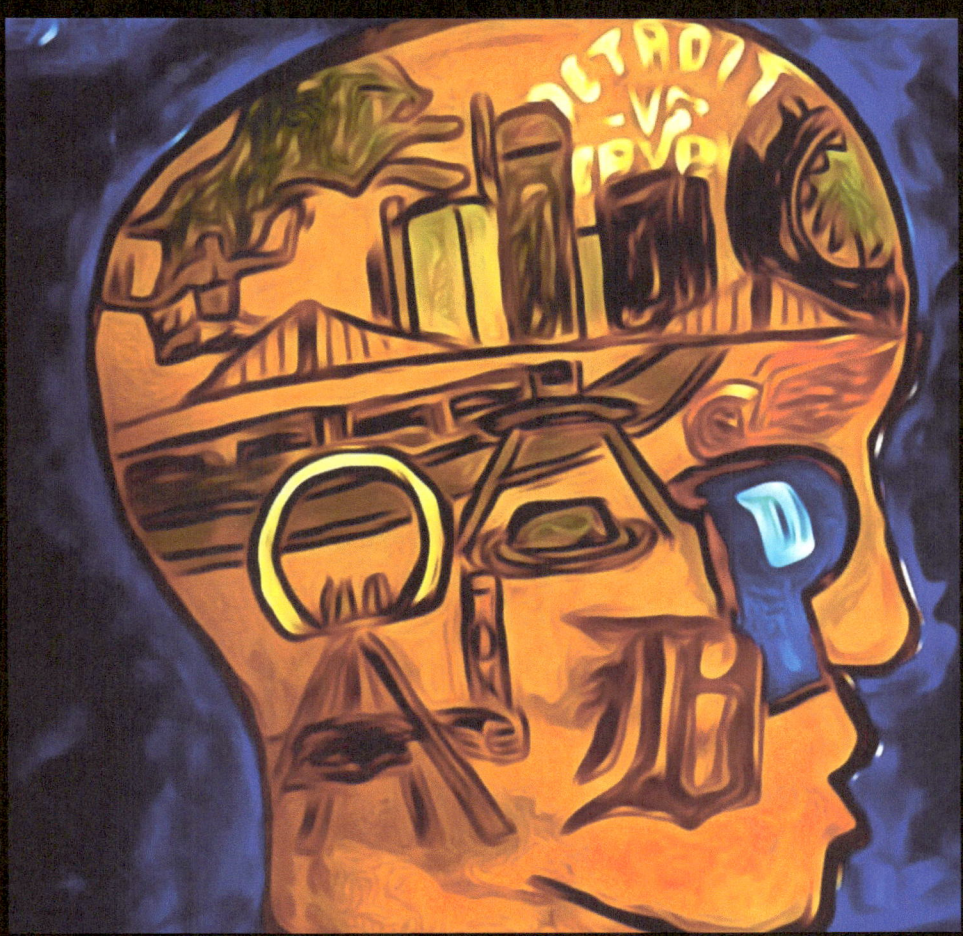

Digital Art. Detroit, Michigan 2016.

Detroit Now

My city is changing

and as I sit and watch

the view isn't the same.

My perspective has been neglected

so, my feelings are mixed.

My home looks different than before.

Million dollar condos

but my family and friends are still poor.

Abandoned.

Lost.

Forgotten.

Left in desolate neighborhoods

that once were affluent communities.

Searching for unity in the midst controversy.

Financial woes

Taking a toll

We were supposed to be the model

The 60s brought

Innovation and riots

broken souls and unpaved roads.

Police brutality and racial tensions

had the city submerged in violence.

Left for dead in hotels

and on the side of roads.

After the tanks and army men left

we were left

left to suffer.

She is...

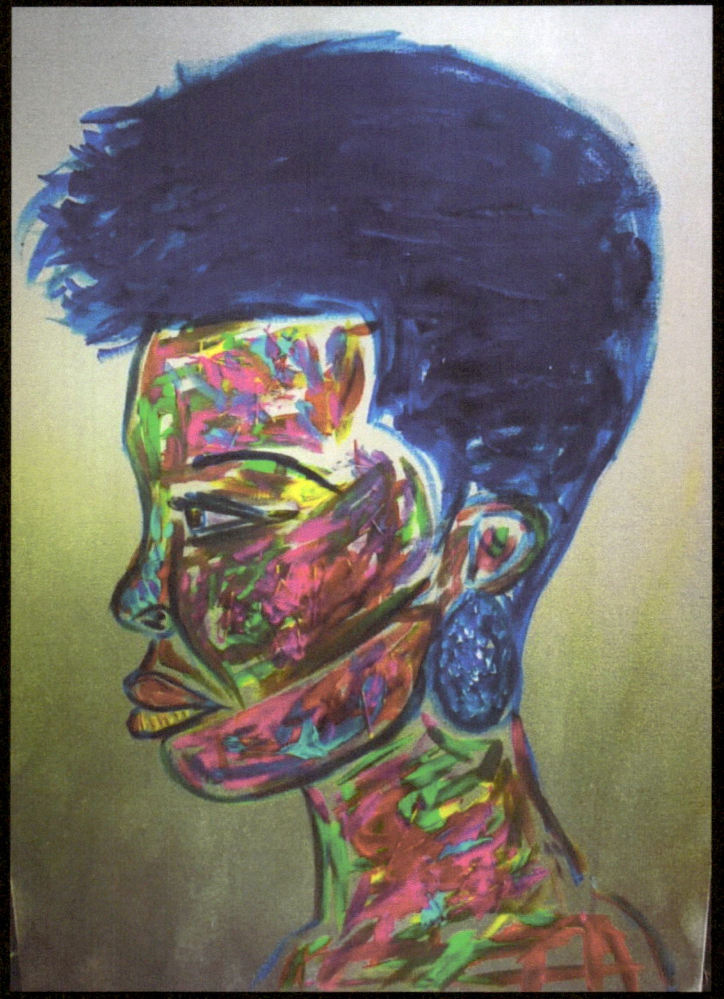

Acrylic painting on canvas. 24 in x 36 in.

Redford, Michigan 2017.

More than Sex

She is so much more

more than

twerking

working in strip clubs

and standing on corners

In 9-inch heels.

She is so much more

more than

double standards

body modifications

explicit words

and curves.

She is so much more

more than

cooking

cleaning

and dreaming of pleasing

YOU.

She is so much more...

more than

rape

domestic violence

and abuse.

She is so much more...

more than

Inequality

unequal pay

and discrimination.

This woman

Is so much more.

No justice! No Peace!

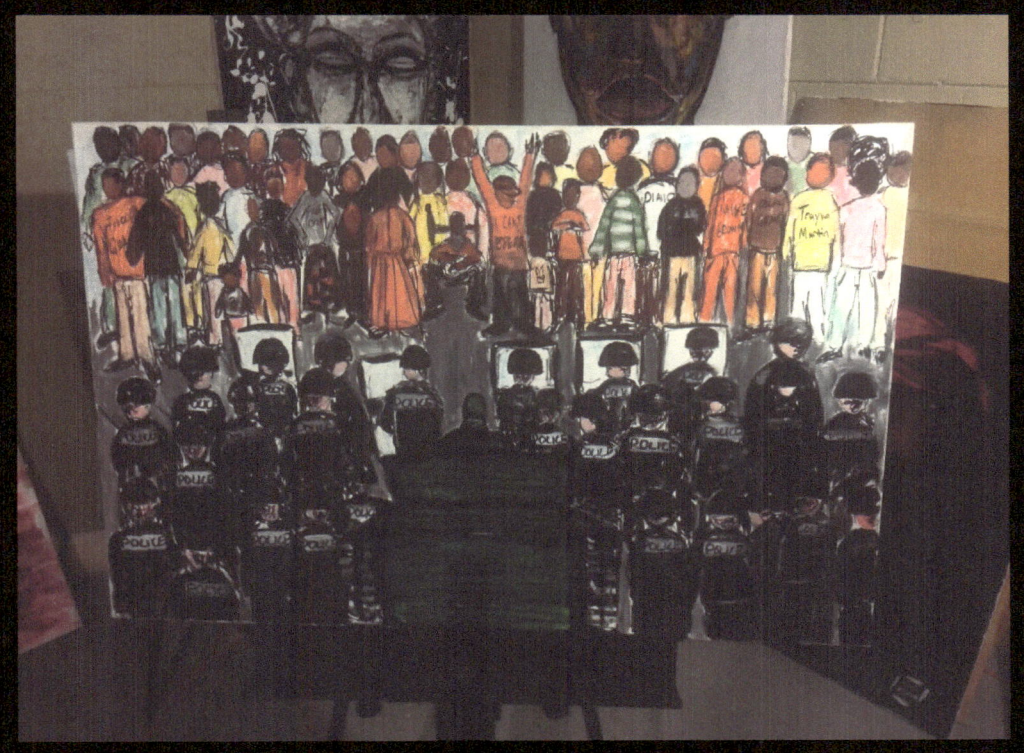

Acrylic painting on canvas. 24 in x 36 in.

Detroit, Michigan 2015.

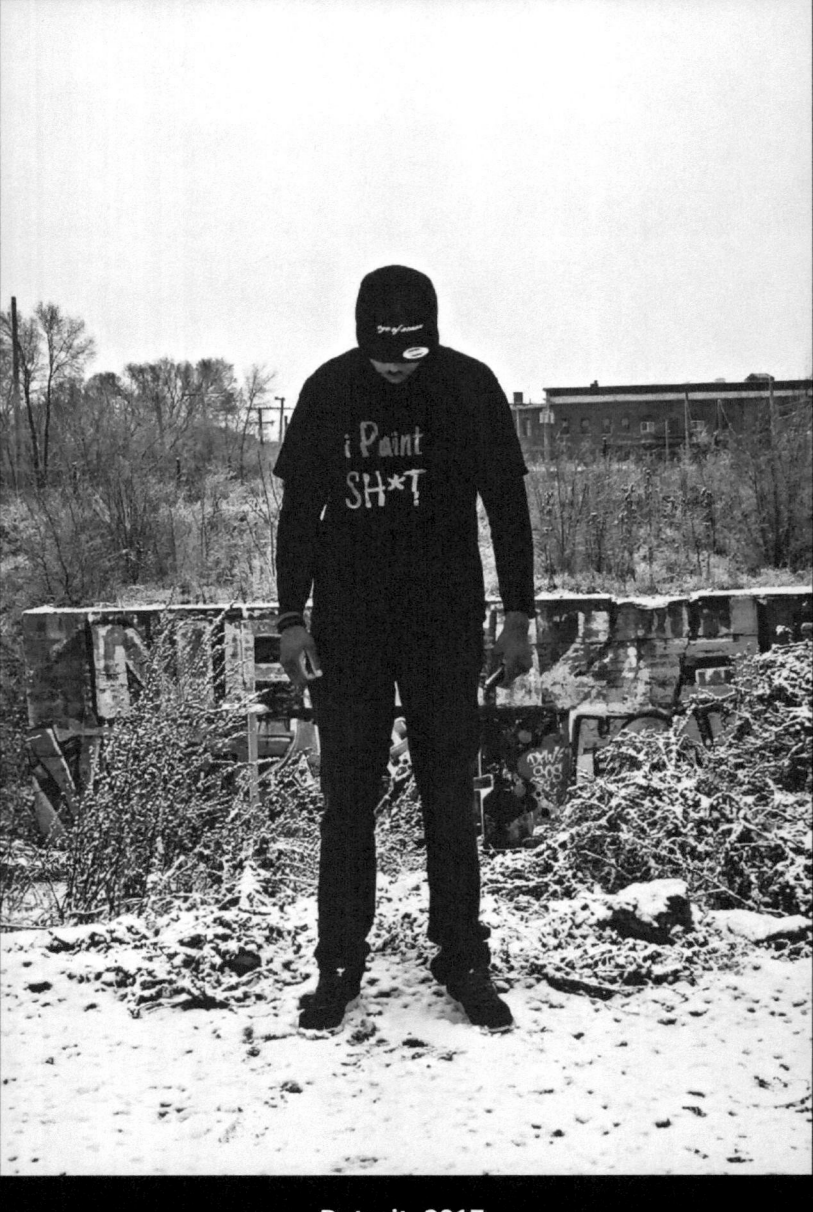

Detroit, 2017.

FLY aWAY

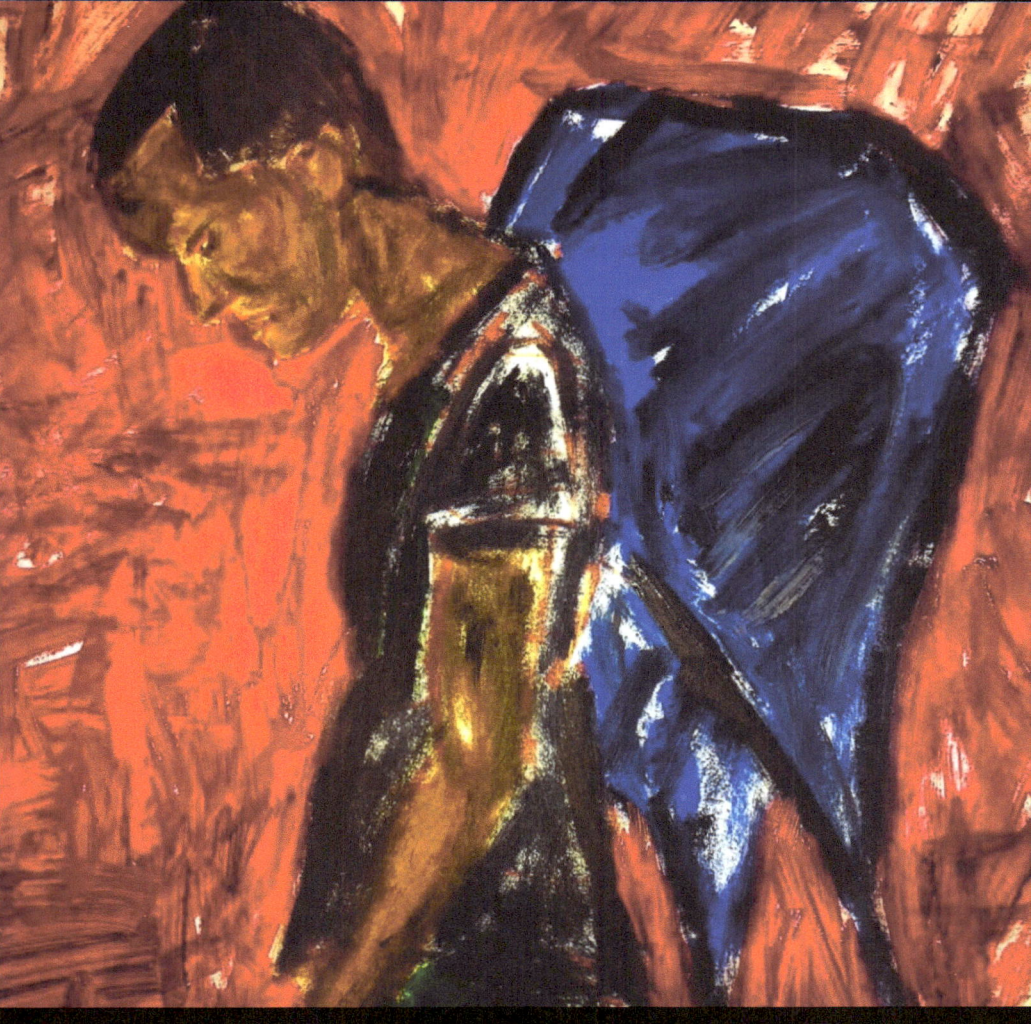

Oil painting on Canson, Mix-Media paper. 11 in x 14 in.

Redford, Michigan 2016.

Fly!

I wish I could fly

go to heaven and ask GOD

to borrow a pair of wings

so I can end wars

reverse the generational curse

to end the continuous cycle

that circles around the world.

I would

restart history

re-write Genesis

be there before Adam and Eve

Osiris and Isis

the Egyptians and Pharaoh's.

Be there before God said

let there be light.

I wish

I wish I could fly

go to heaven and ask GOD

to borrow a pair of wings

so I can

rewind time

change minds

make the world more equal

make money obsolete

stop the slave trade

Manifest Destiny

and Apartheid

So, my people can continue to rise.

I wish

I wish I could fly

go to heaven and ask GOD

to borrow a pair of wings

so I can

reconstruct my community

breathe life into the lifeless

rebuild the minds of those lost

paint pictures of hope in every hood and every ghetto.

I wish

I wish I could fly

go to heaven and ask GOD

to borrow a pair of wings

bring back Malcolm and Martin

tell him that the little boys and girls

are still starving

for food

for knowledge

for Help

and we still need you.

I wish

I wish I could fly

go to heaven and ask God

to borrow a pair of wings

so I can live in the sky

learn the truth

meet my ancestors

talk to Harriet

ask her what would she do.

I wish

I wish I could fly

go to heaven and ask God

to borrow a pair of wings

bring my grandma back

tell her I love her

take the cancer from my Uncle's body

see my mama smile everyday

I wish.

I wish I could fly

go to heaven and ask God

to borrow a pair of wings

so things could be different

so people can experience love

so the world can be at peace

And we can all live free

I wish.

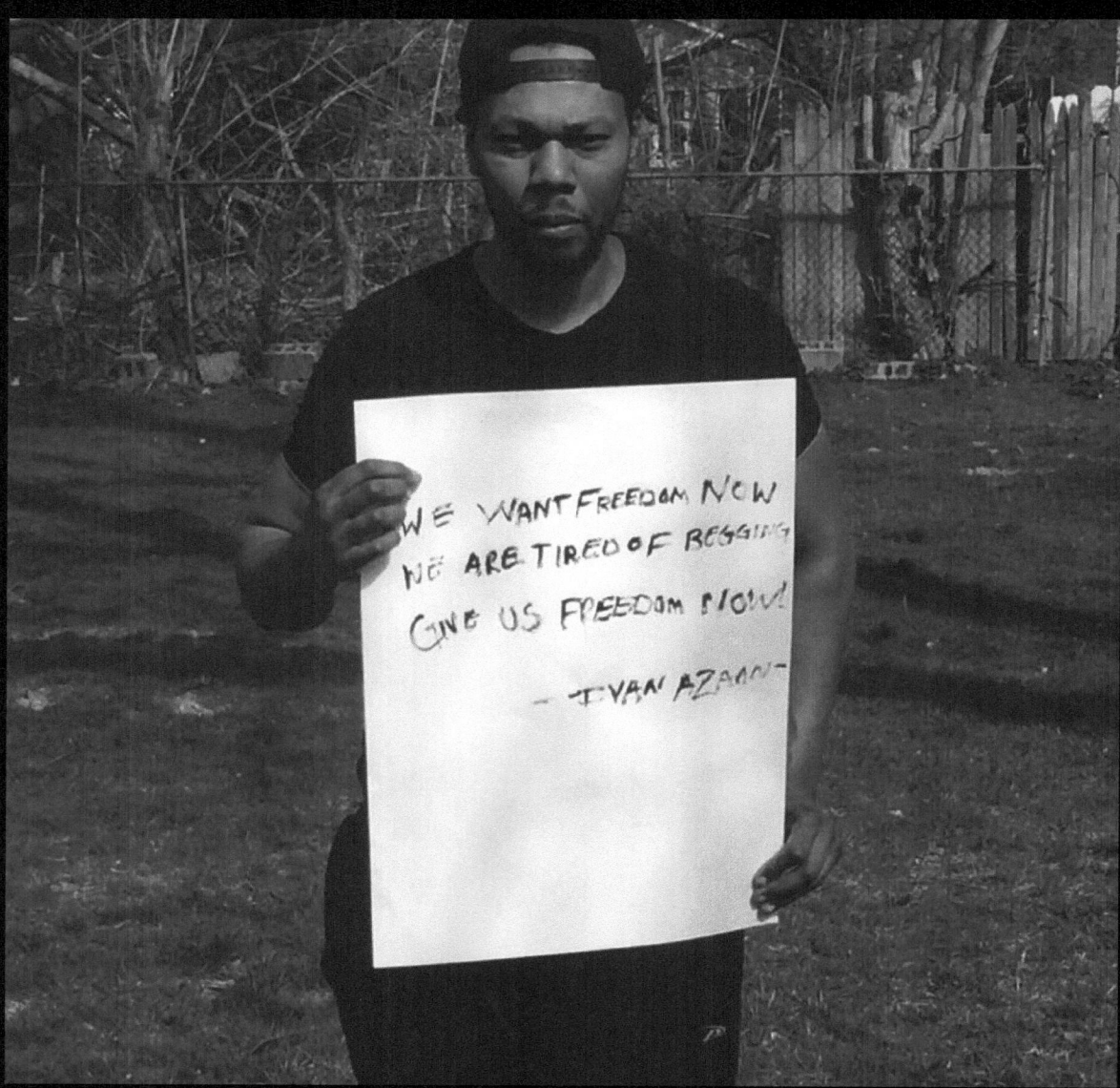

Redford Michigan, 2017.

African Pride

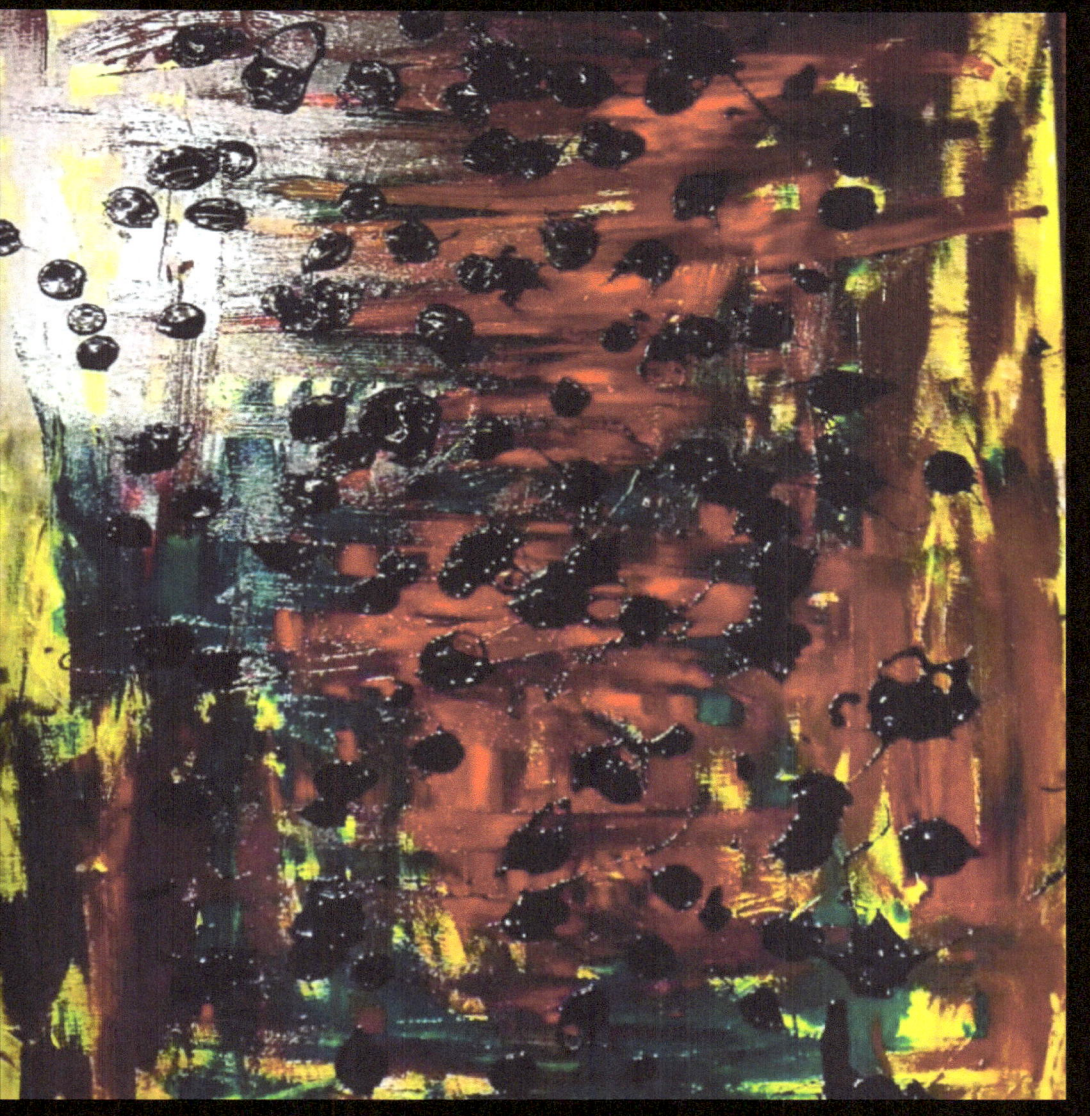

Acrylic painting on canvas. 24 in x 36 in.

Redford, Michigan 2016.

Proud to BE

Big nose

Big lips

Big teeth.

Scars on my hands

On my knees

And my feet.

Brown skin

Perfect blend

I AM ME.

LETTERS ◀

Detroit Free Press

It's up to us, not politicians, to fix Detroit

I am a 27-year-old black male from Detroit. I love my city with all my heart. It's hard to watch the news and hear about the bad things going in Detroit. I recently left Detroit and moved to Texas. I left for the same reasons most people leave. I wanted to seek better opportunities and an overall better life. It was one of the hardest decisions I have ever made. It's especially hard because I didn't plan to "run away" from the city I love because life was rough. My plan was to fight for a better Detroit, and do my part while living there. Even though I live in Texas, I keep Detroit in my heart.

People often ask me, why do you love Detroit so much? I think Detroit has the recipe for unity. People from all backgrounds and walks of life are giving back. Go downtown, or to the Brightmoor community and look at the things that are going on. There are so many beautiful gardens, murals and businesses opening up. A lot of people try to depict the city as this third-world country.

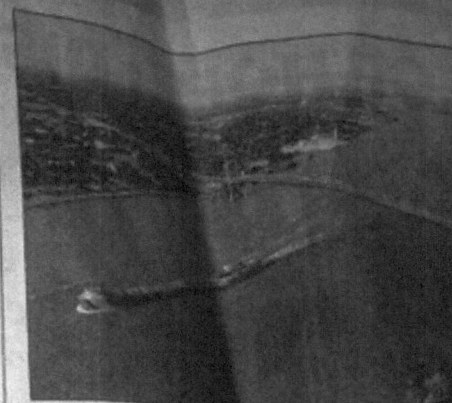

For safety reasons, certain hazardous materials ar the Ambassador Bridge. ROMAIN BLANQUART/DETROIT F

Detroit is a place where hope for a brighter tomorrow lives. Instead of all the negative talk, try being uplifting or doing something to help Detroit out. We understand the problem, now we have to fix it. It can't just depend on the politicians to save our city, we have to — the people.

Ivan Tarver
Haltom City, Texas

Why up r to help a

Ambass Manuel (M pushing h 84-year-o protects and our structur allow h cross t

Fir spond be dif

Haltom City, Texas 2014.

Black Lives

I'm tired of seeing brothers

get murdered

PERIOD.

No question

Just tired.

Beyond Bothered

scared to be a father.

FREEDOM NOW!

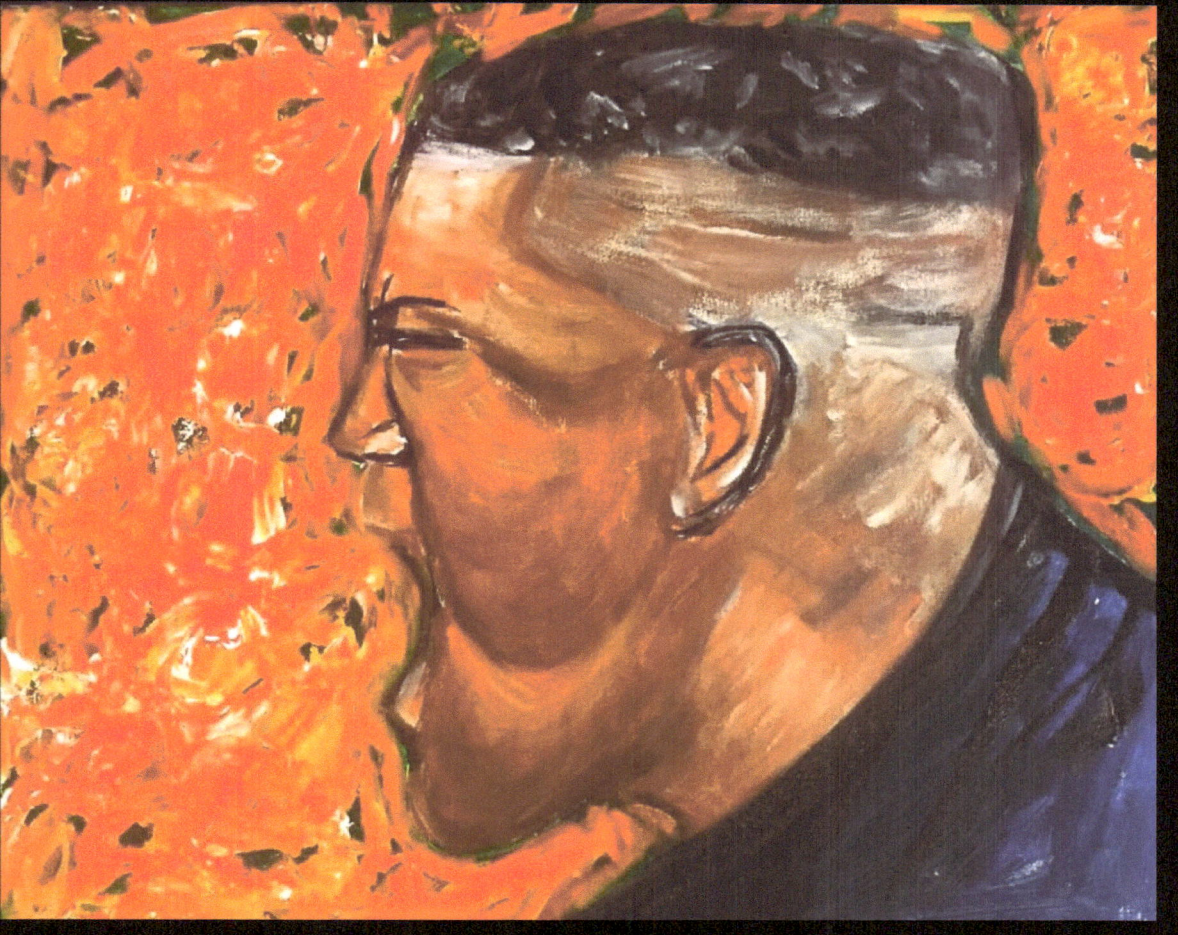

Acrylic painting on canvas. 16 in x 20 in.

Detroit, Michigan 2017.

Modern Day STRUGGLE

We were convicted at birth

enlisted into a country

with bloody hands and deceitful plans.

Since the beginning we have been told lies

we have always had the ability to fly like eagles

we just never believed in our wings

and our dreams.

We are

talented, beautiful and educated.

The possibilities for us

are unlimited,

but our thoughts

remain limited.

We are suffering

willie lynch

wearing invisible chains.

The combinations that lock our brain

remain.

No cure for the pain

And the years of suffrage.

We are still searching for freedom In 2018.

Prototype B

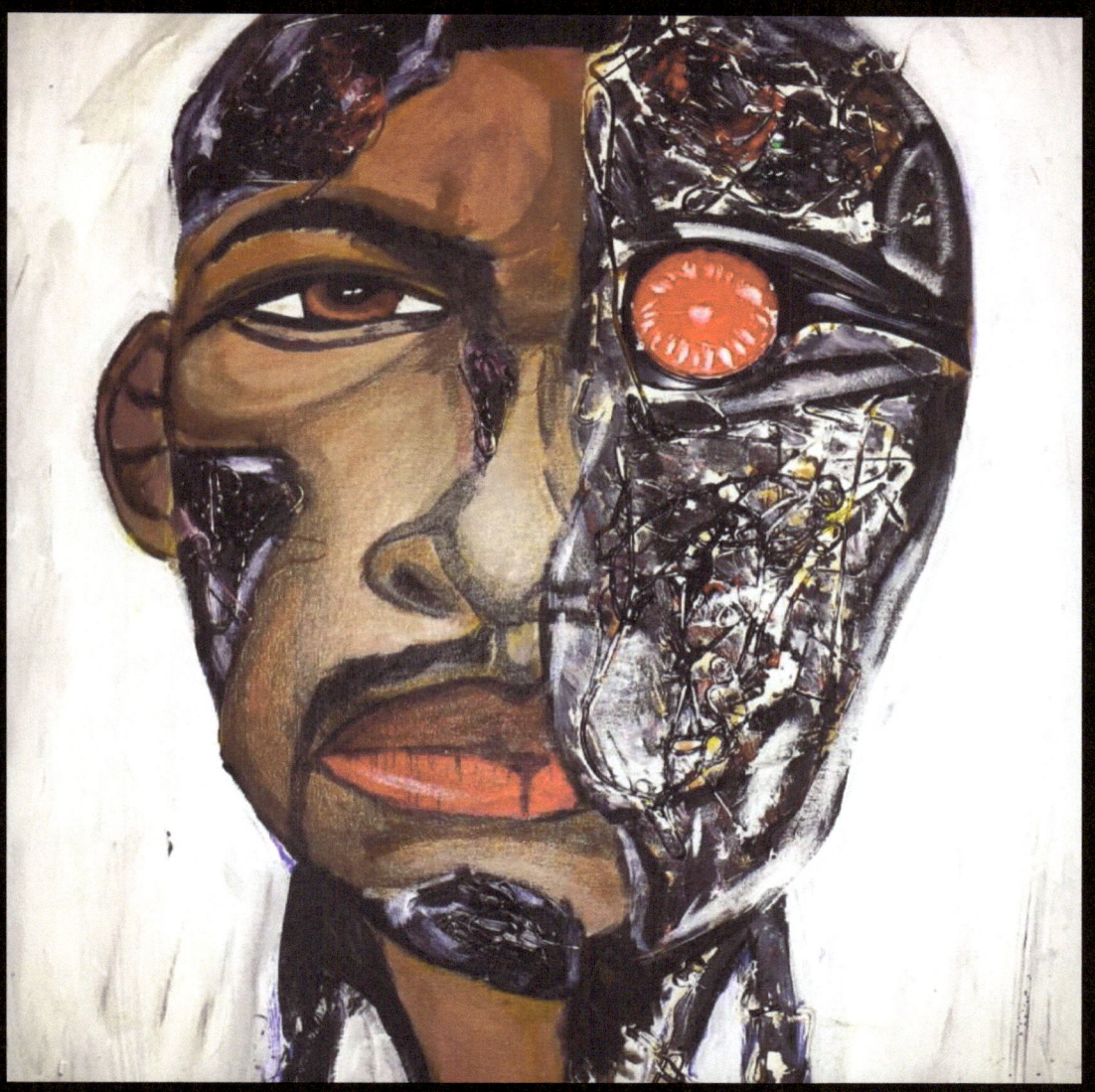

Mixed Media painting on canvas. 16in X 20in.

Chicago, Illinois 2010.

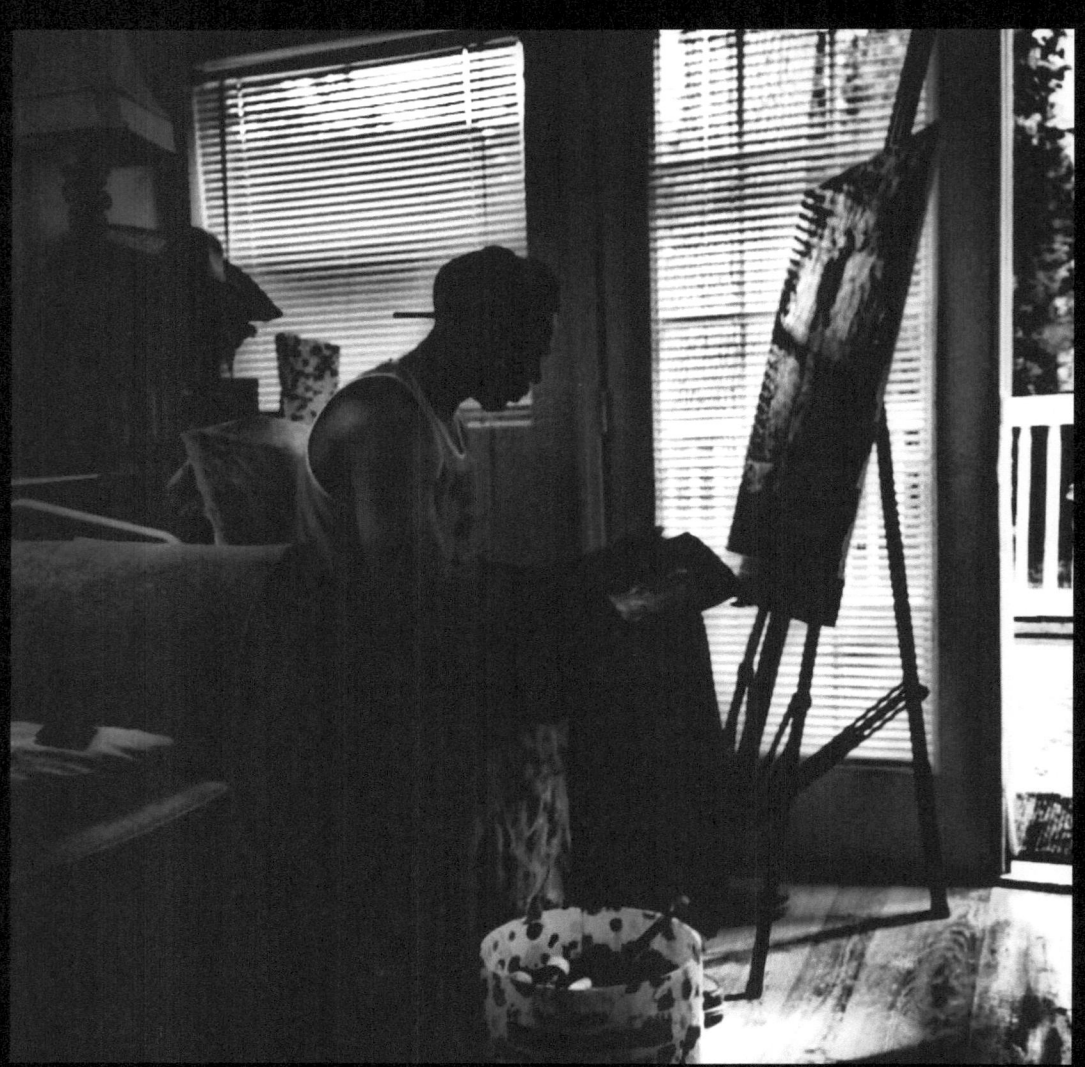

Detroit, Michigan 2016.

Kalief

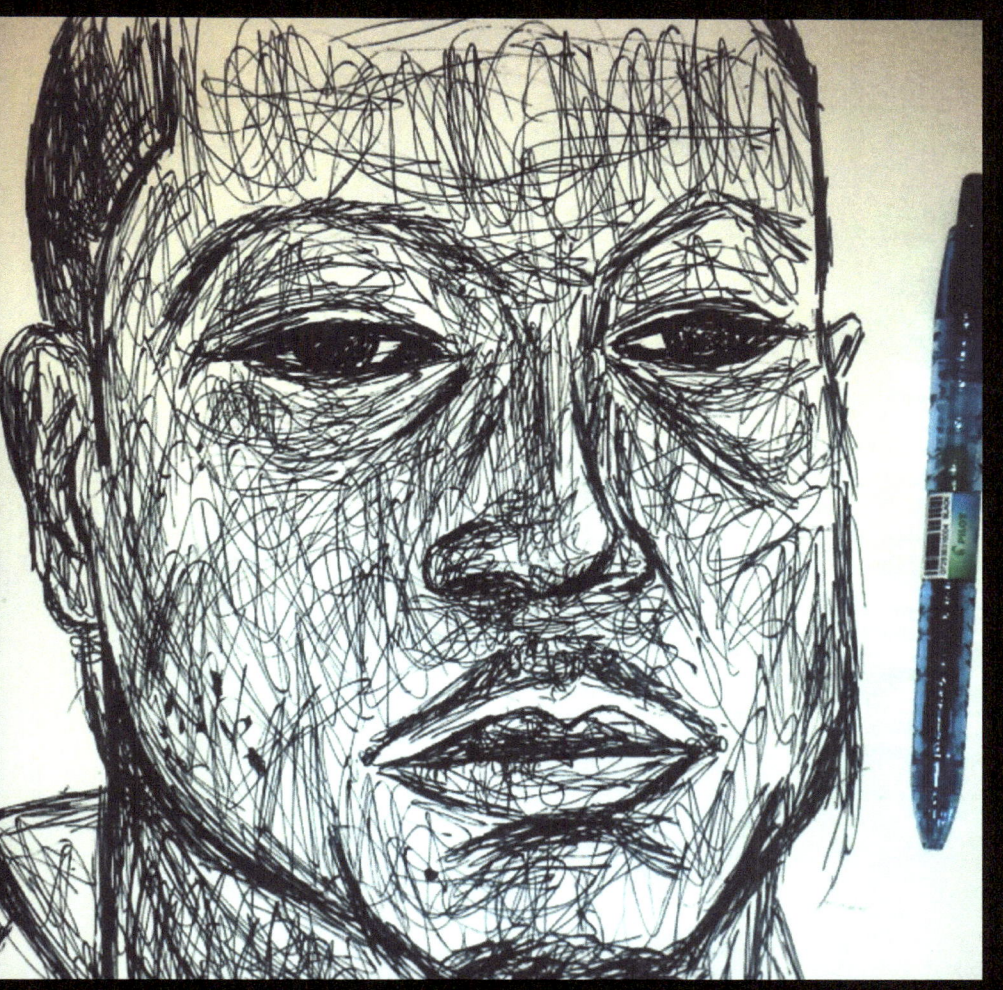

Pen drawing on Canson, Mix-Media paper. 11 in x 14 in.

Redford, Michigan 2017.

Brother Kalief

3 years

suffering

stuck

In a cage

where lions play.

Convicted of nothing

living behind cold bars.

They watched

as you were beaten

and ripped of your innocence

they questioned your mental health

but never question our justice system.

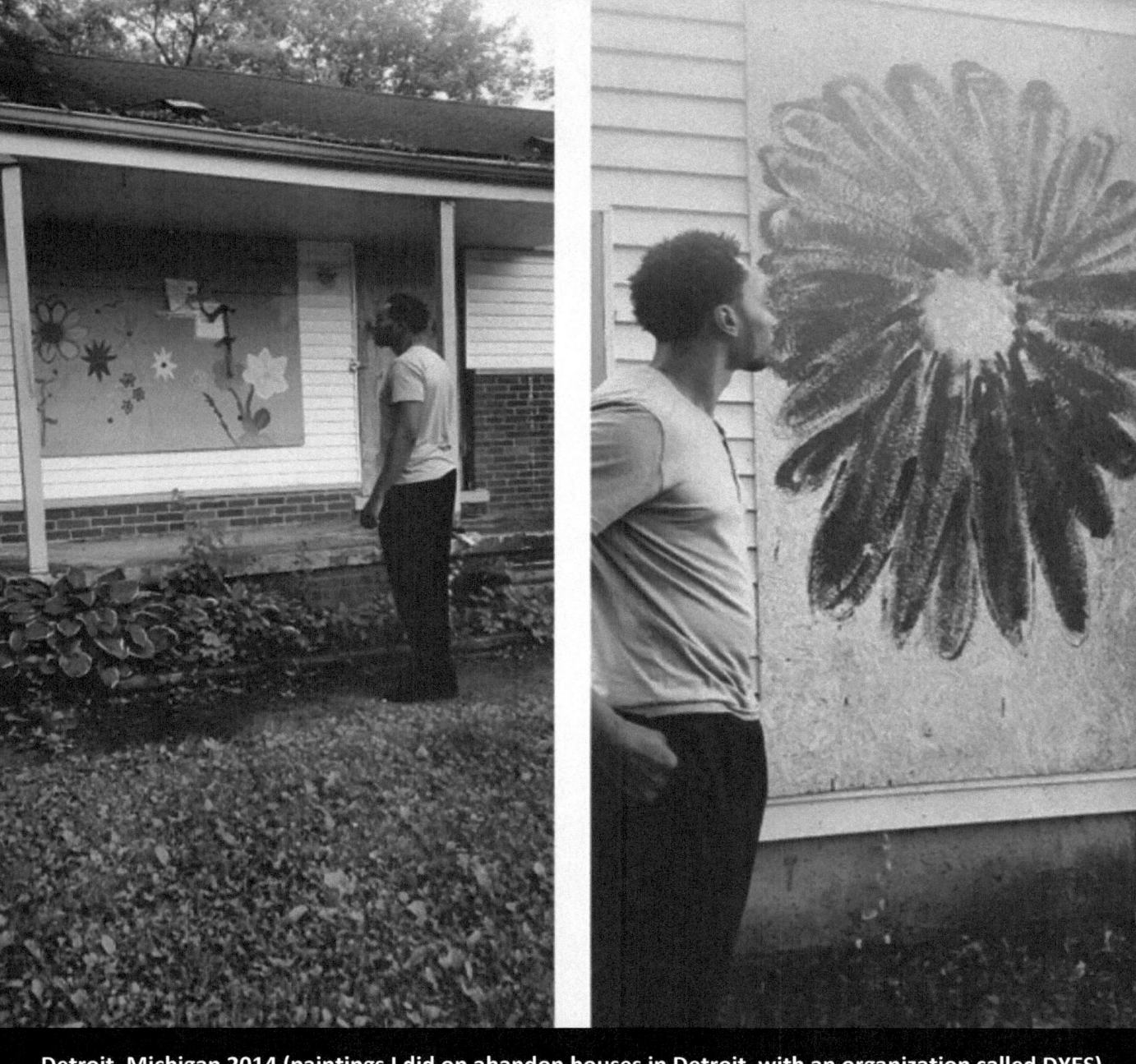

Detroit, Michigan 2014 (paintings I did on abandon houses in Detroit, with an organization called DYES).

Pray for my city

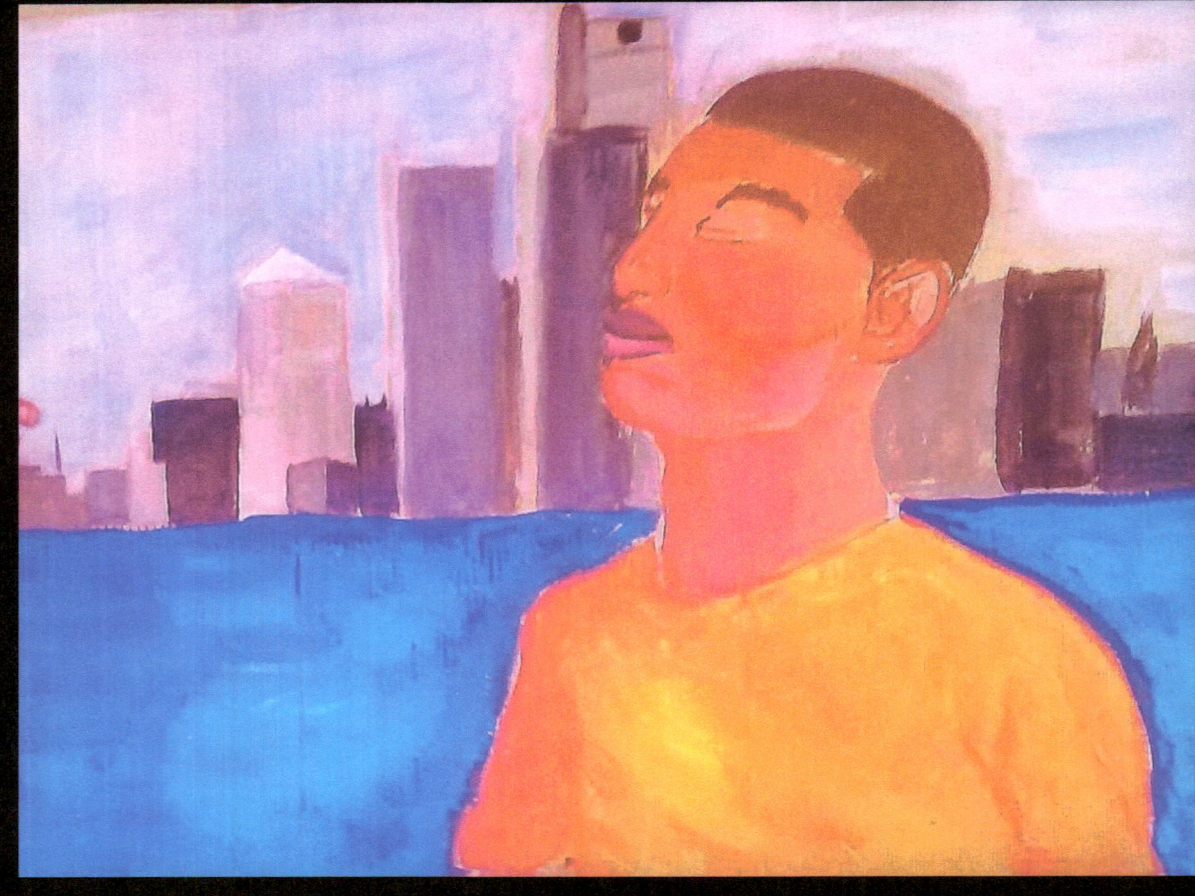

Acrylic painting on cardboard. 20 in X 16 in.

Fort Worth, Texas 2013.

Drunk in Love

Intoxicated by your love

It's because of you

I almost lost it all.

I felt like I needed you.

There's nothing I wouldn't do for you.

You were my best friend.

It seemed like our love would never end.

I was hypnotized

by the consumption of you.

With every sip

my lips quivered.

I became numb

and nothing mattered.

I valued the constant laughter.

When we were together

you brought me joy and bliss.

I was addicted to your kiss.

You kept me high.

I felt like I became one with the sky.

I was living a fantasy

with no responsibility.

Limitless.

Hurting everybody

including myself.

All because of you.

You kept me coming back

until that night

when everything turned Black

and I didn't remember.

It was almost December.

cold nights

And fights

with my demons

almost pushed me over the edge.

I had two choices

change or continue.

For me

Change was the only thing on the menu.

Energy

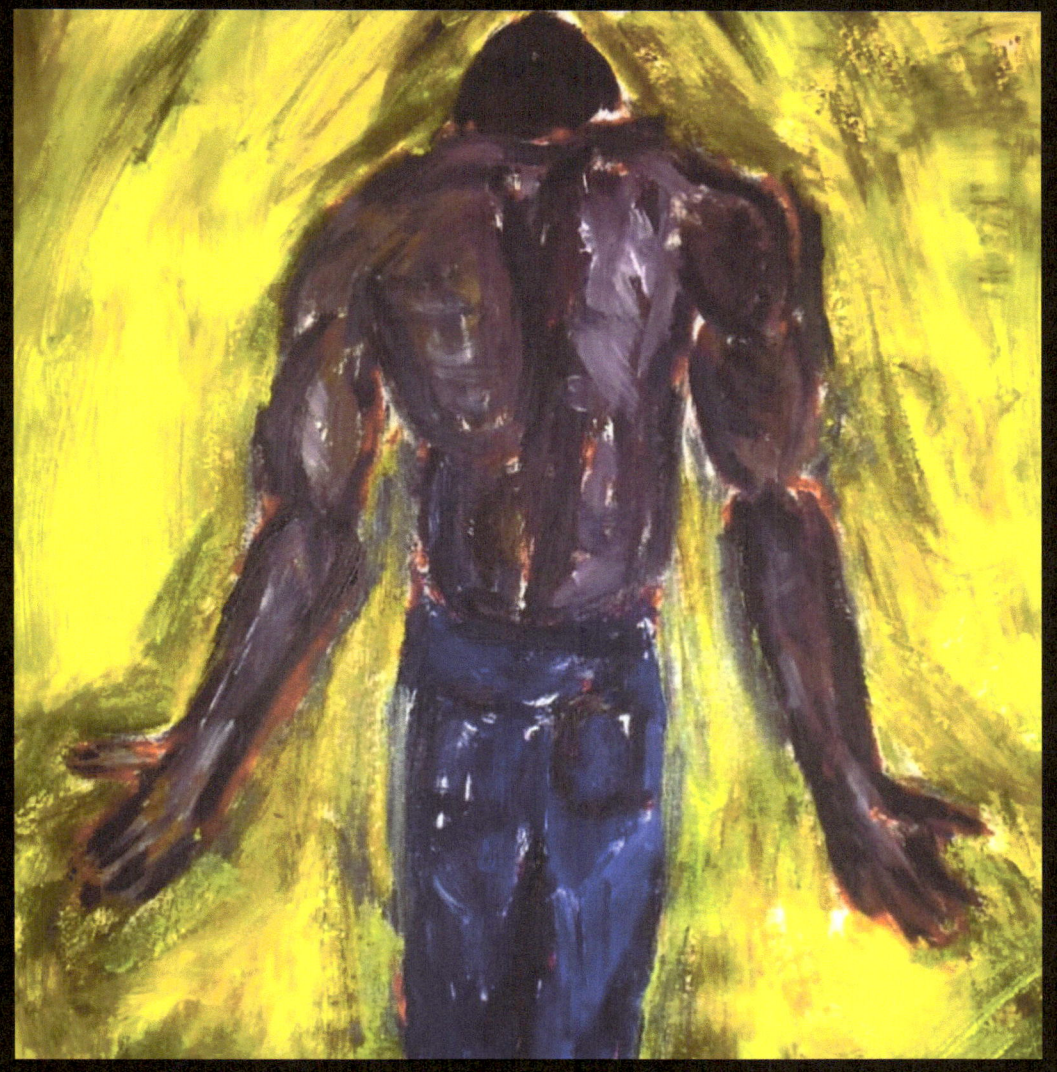

Oil painting on Canson, Mix-Media paper. 18 in x 24 in.

Redford, Michigan 2017.

WISDOM

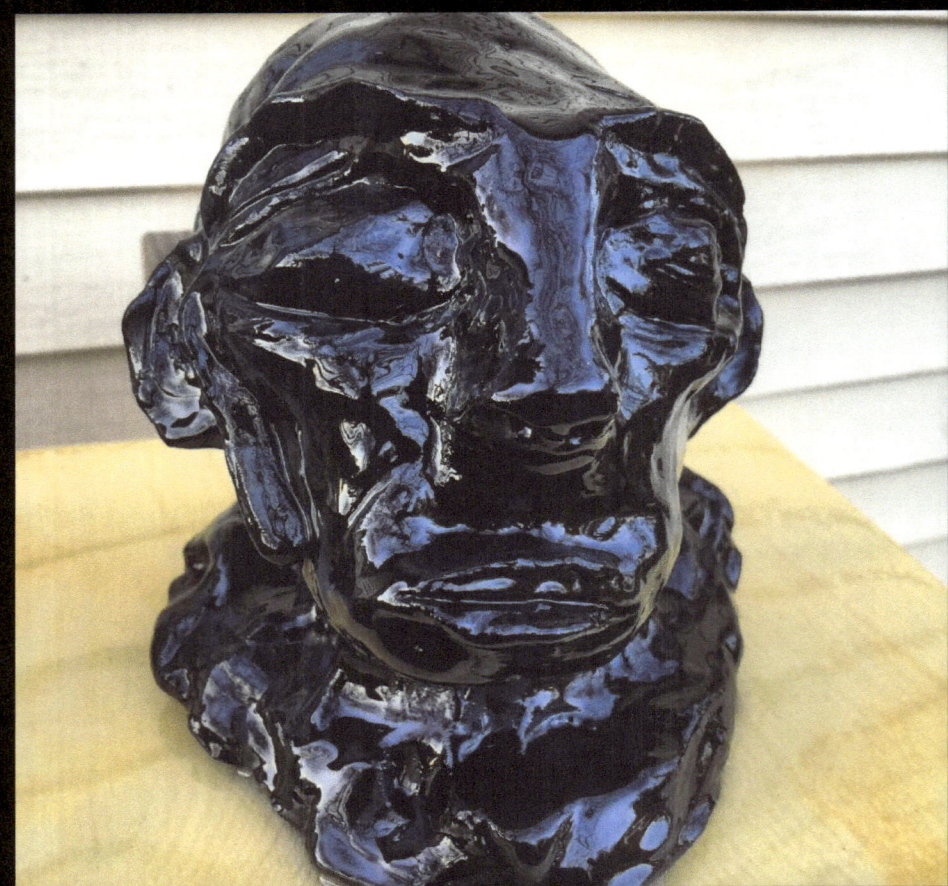

Healing

Open wounds

never heal in the midst

of constant trauma.

Stitches never repair

the hurt and the pain

that puncture souls

and leave scars

On fragile skin.

There's no restoration

In a field of complacent thoughts.

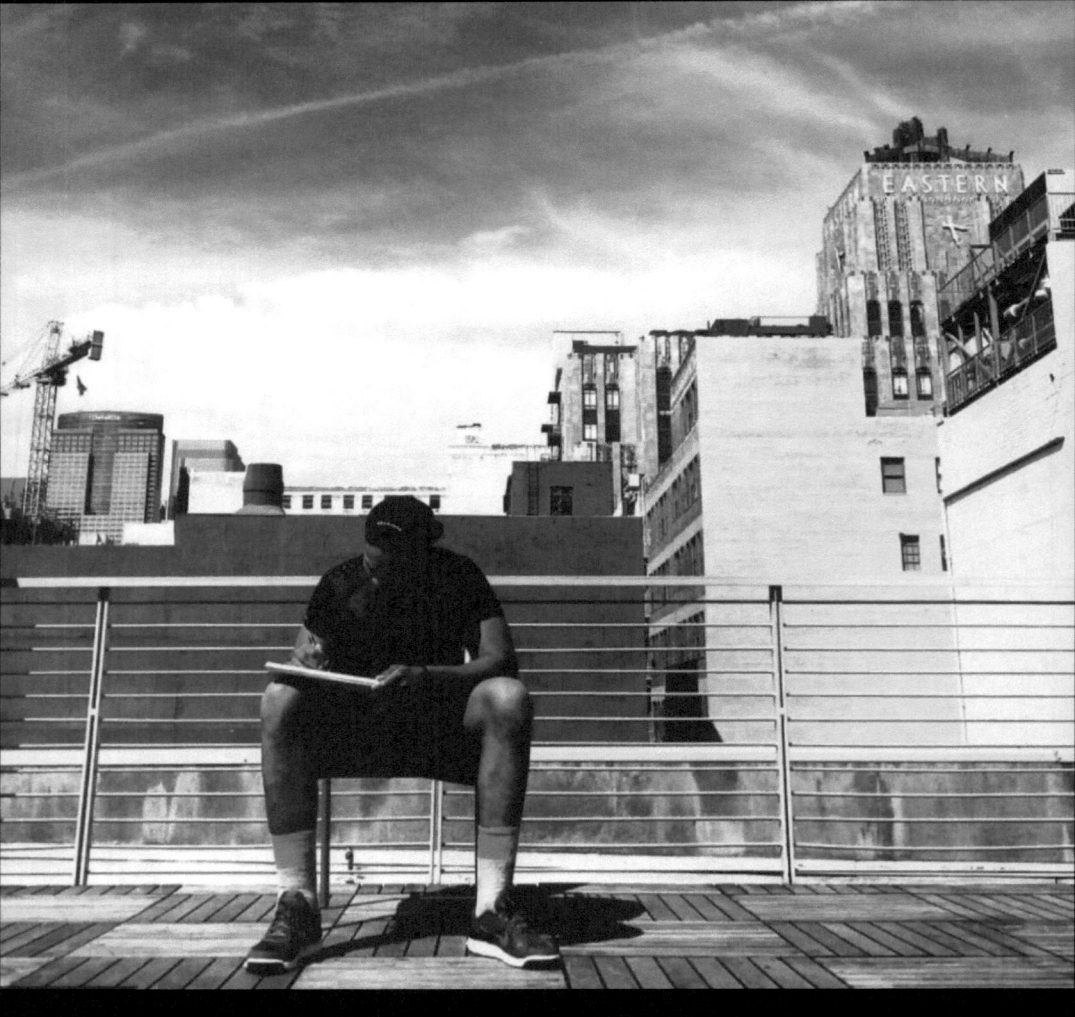

Los Angeles, California 2017.

FIRE INSIDE

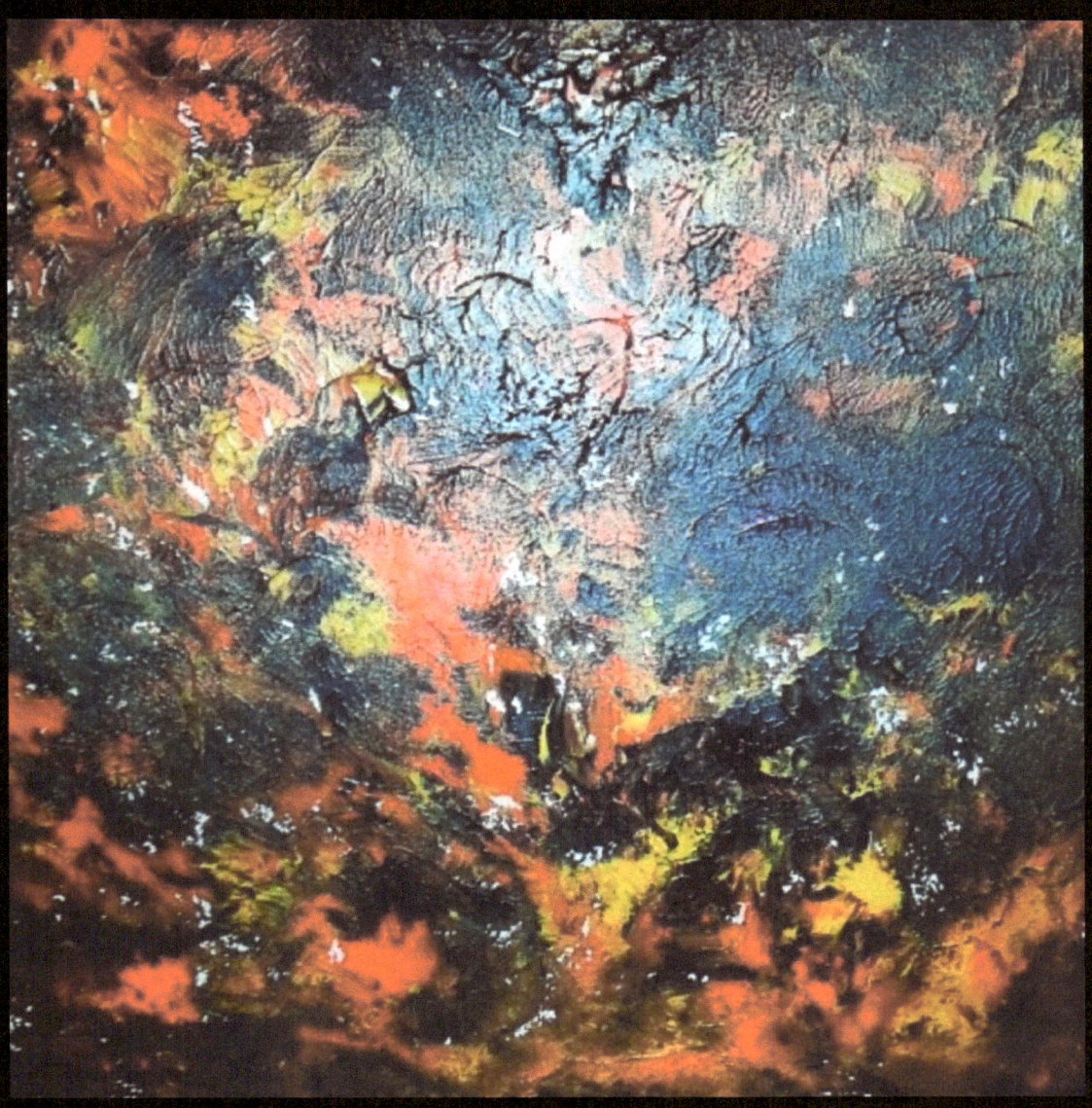

Acrylic painting on canvas. 24 in x 36 in.

Detroit, Michigan 2016.

The Fire

The flames flicker

fighting

to make an unwelcoming change.

After all is done

and the flames are no more.

Dark days

distant memories

and bright futures

sit at the forefront.

Change is near.

Red, Black & Green

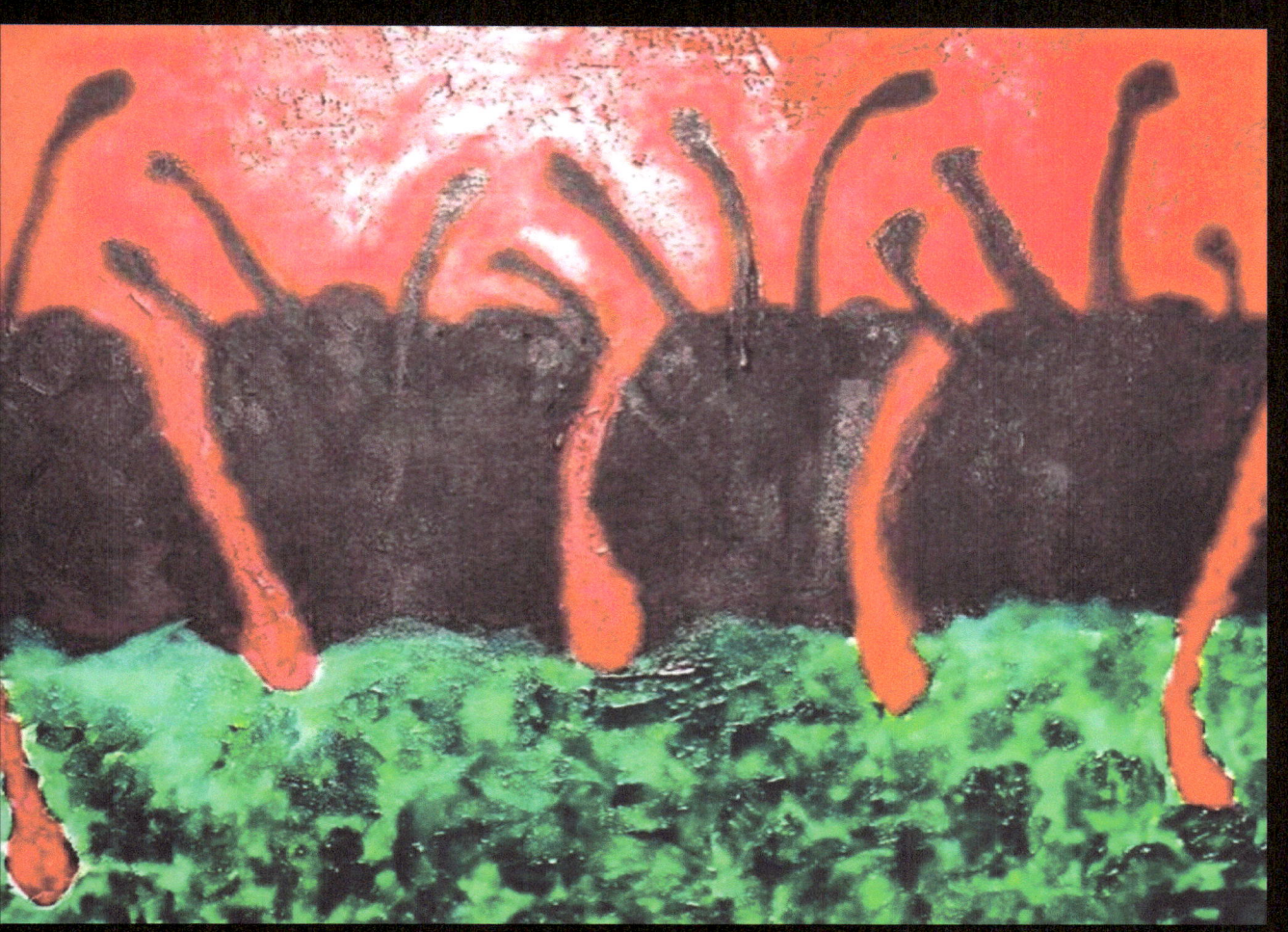

Acrylic painting on canvas. 16 in X 20 in.

Good Ole' Uncle Sam

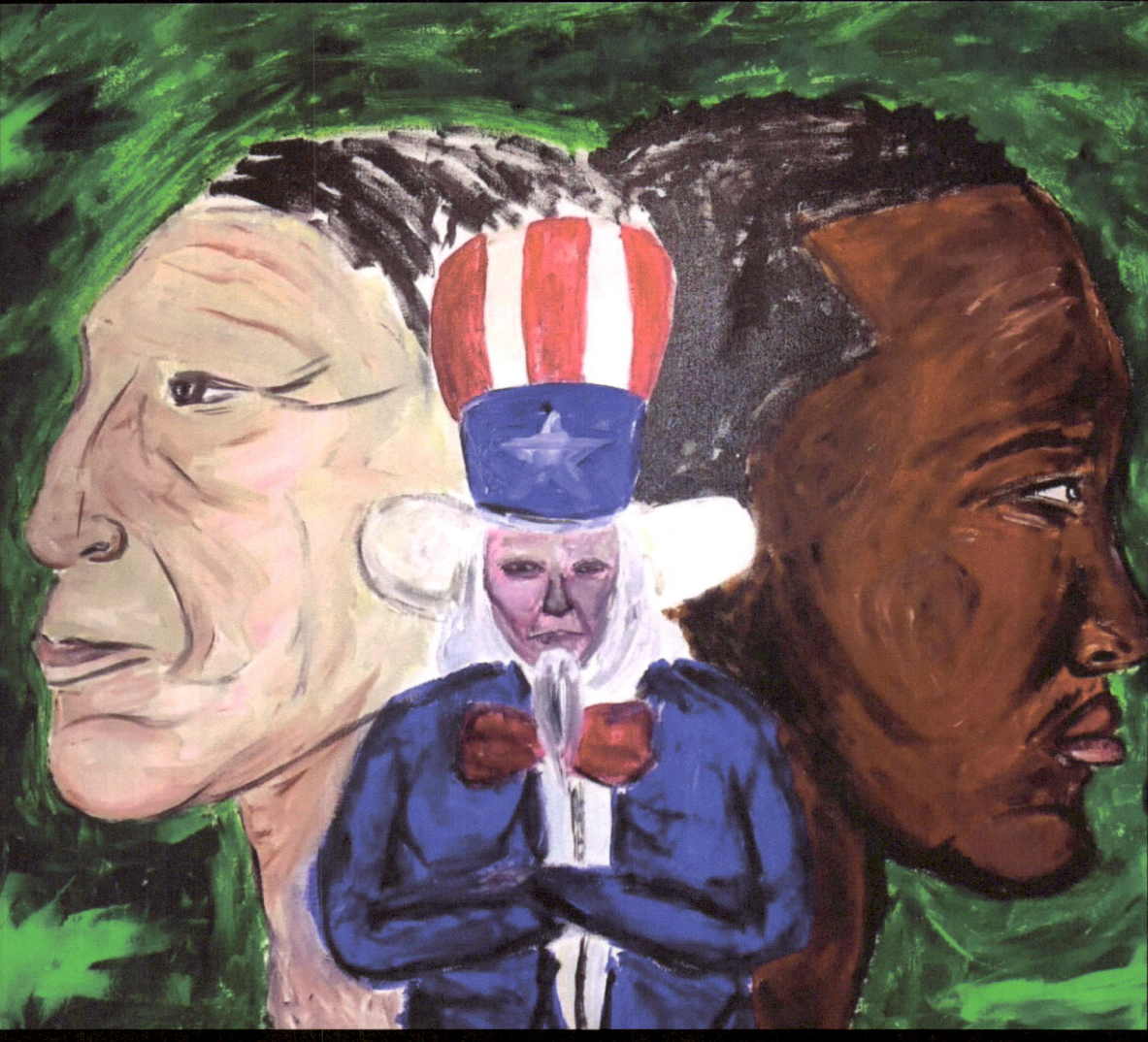

Acrylic painting on canvas. 24 in x 36 in.

Redford, Michigan 2017.

MY Country

I live in a country

where we are still striving

with blistered hands and knees

Still.

Singing songs.

Holding signs.

seeking rights.

Where everything is Black and White.

Still.

We pray to Christ

expecting the unexpected

while living in a neglected space

far away from dreams

but we reach for the stars

Still.

Hopin' to get a piece of light.

To help brighten our smiles

and make our tomorrows easier.

With our lungs for air

we take deep breaths

Still.

Breathing in pollution.

Sick from living life in lifeless institutions

where our mental help

Isn't helped

Still.

They give us medicine and feed us lies

put us back in society

and expect us to try

Still.

They shrug their shoulders

while we go back to the same life.

The same killing.

The same stealing.

Still

ain't no healin'

just meds

that keep you coming back

spending money

and dying slowly.

Still.

Ain't no help

In my country.

Kneel

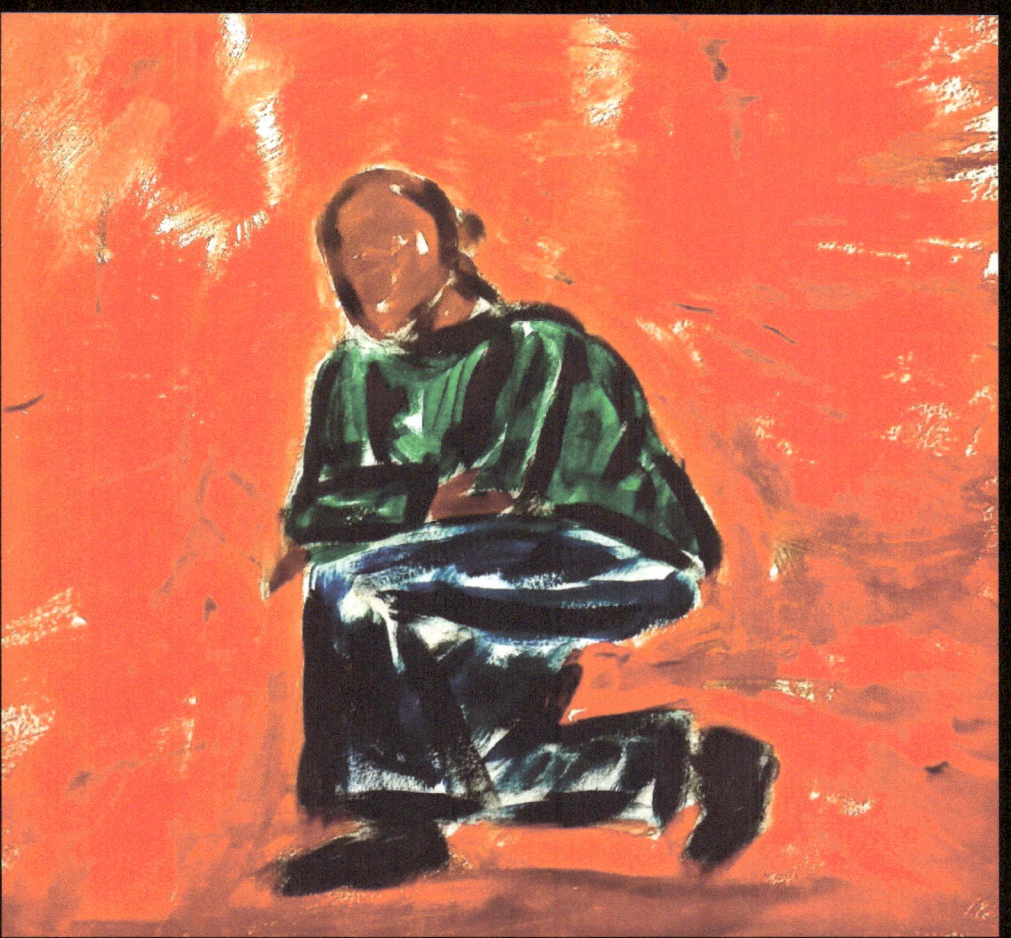

Acrylic painting on Canson, Mix-Media paper. 11 in x 14 in

Redford, Michigan 2017.

Kneel

If you kneel

they will still kill you.

If you stand

they will still kill you.

If you speak

they will still kill you.

Stereotyped

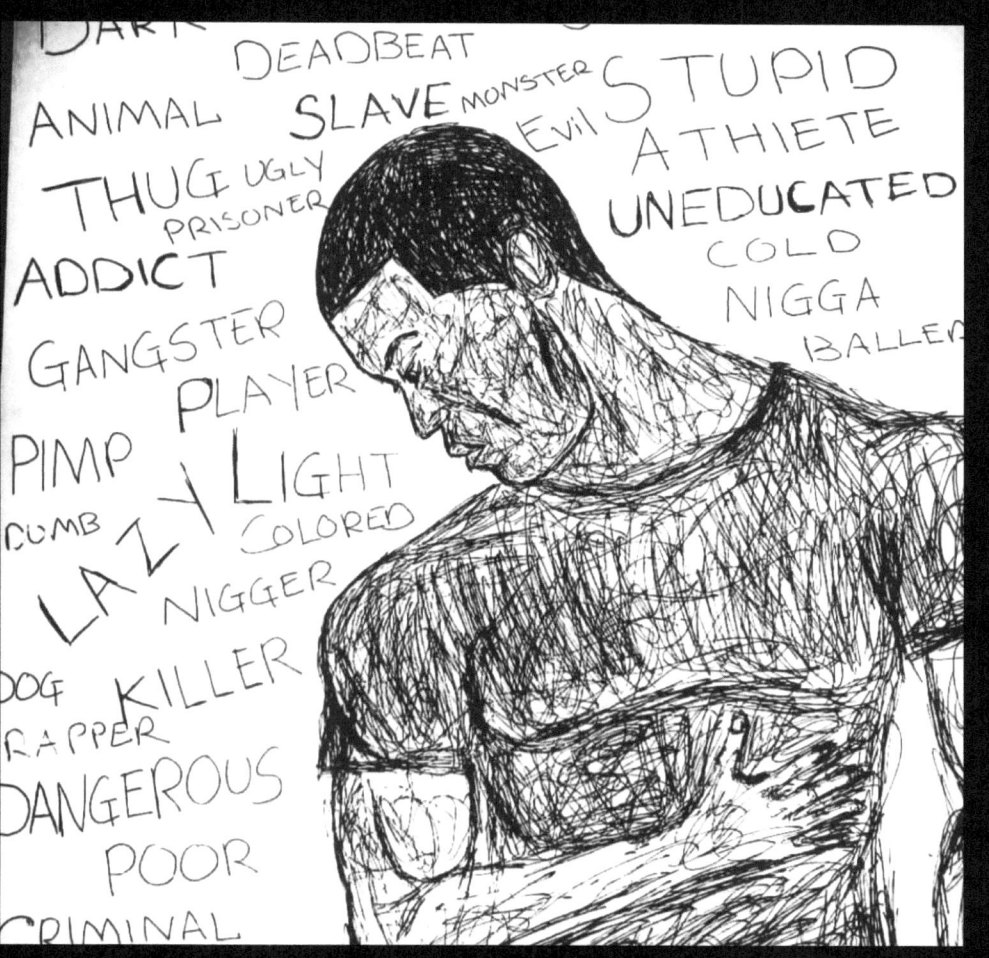

Pen drawing on Canson, Mix-Media paper. 18 in x 24 in.

Detroit, Michigan 2015.

Endangered

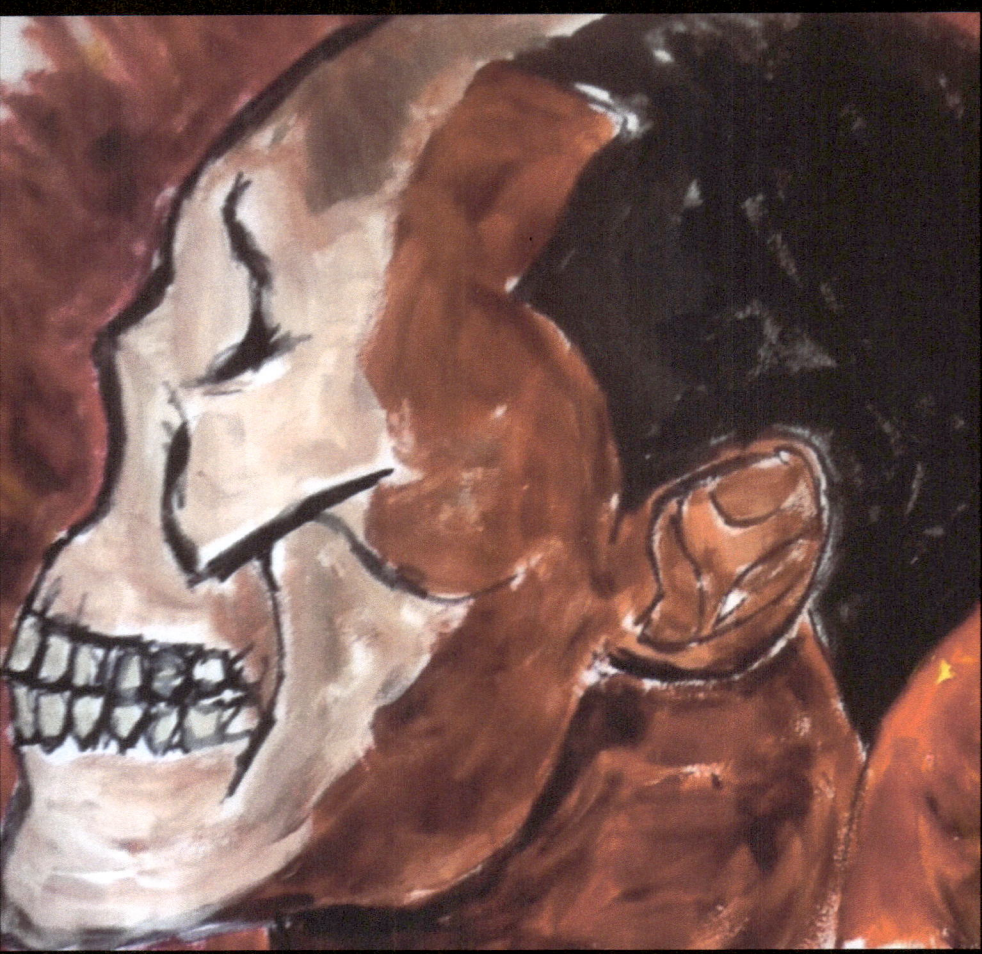

Acrylic painting Canson, Mix-Media paper. 18 in x 24 in.

Invisible Man

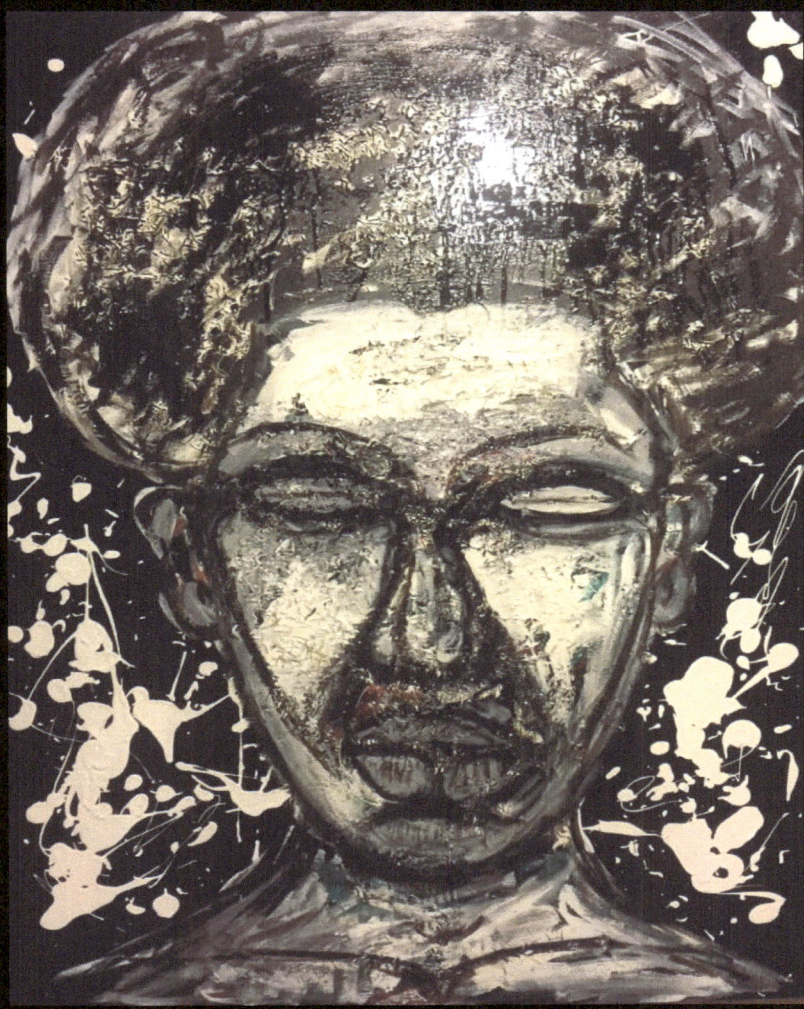

Acrylic painting on canvas. 36 in x 48 in.

Redford, Michigan 2017.

Invisible

Blinded by darkness

My skin kept them confused

They found their answers in my completion

My color made them hesitant

They refused to see me

My words couldn't hide the obvious

They knew me

Before I spoke

They knew me after they called me

Nigger.

Black History Mural

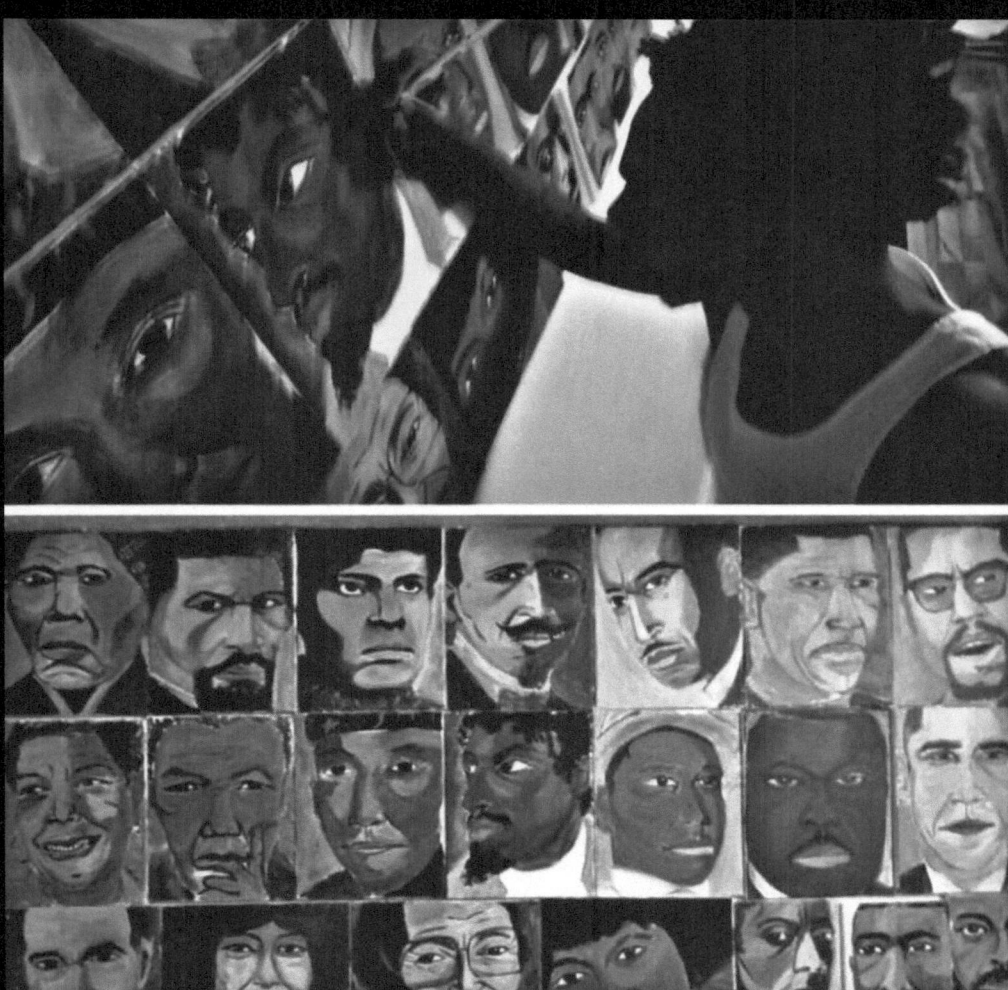

Chicago, Illinois 2010.

Writers Block

I haven't written like this in about 8 years

I was trapped in my mind

Confined

to over thinking and drinking

Sipping' on memories of infancy

Baby boy

I was my mama's youngest

Ahead of my time

Nicknamed prime

No 21

But I'm something like a savage

Young king

sittin' on the throne

with something that look like Isis

God in the flesh

I know she got my back in a crisis

When it comes to letting that thang ride

Baby girl the nicest

She got me back writing

Got me back fighting

Like Claude McKay

If we must die

Let it be noble

Not lying face down in the street

By the hands of the po po

I speak the truth

Give you the roots

Straight from the scalp

So you can see where we started

Str8t from the bottom

Next to the skeletons that no longer live in the closet

I lost so many homies

So many people in the struggle

That tried to become millionaires off the hustle

Selling rocks to indentured servants

Serving time in alleys and on corners

Glued to the street

Glued to defeat

Different day

Same shit

But we still got to eat

And digest the rest

They say look to the sky

You should know that you're blessed

But it's all about perspective

Because as a shorty I was neglected

So my vision is a little blurry

Most of the shorties on my block were potential

Steph curry's

Letting that thang fly from

Anywhere on the court

But when we end up in court

They convict us

Lynch us

This is a process

It started from birth

What's a Black life worth?

They pay you money for your soul

Give you pennies and a body of henny

Then tell you turn up

While they sit back and watch.

The Key

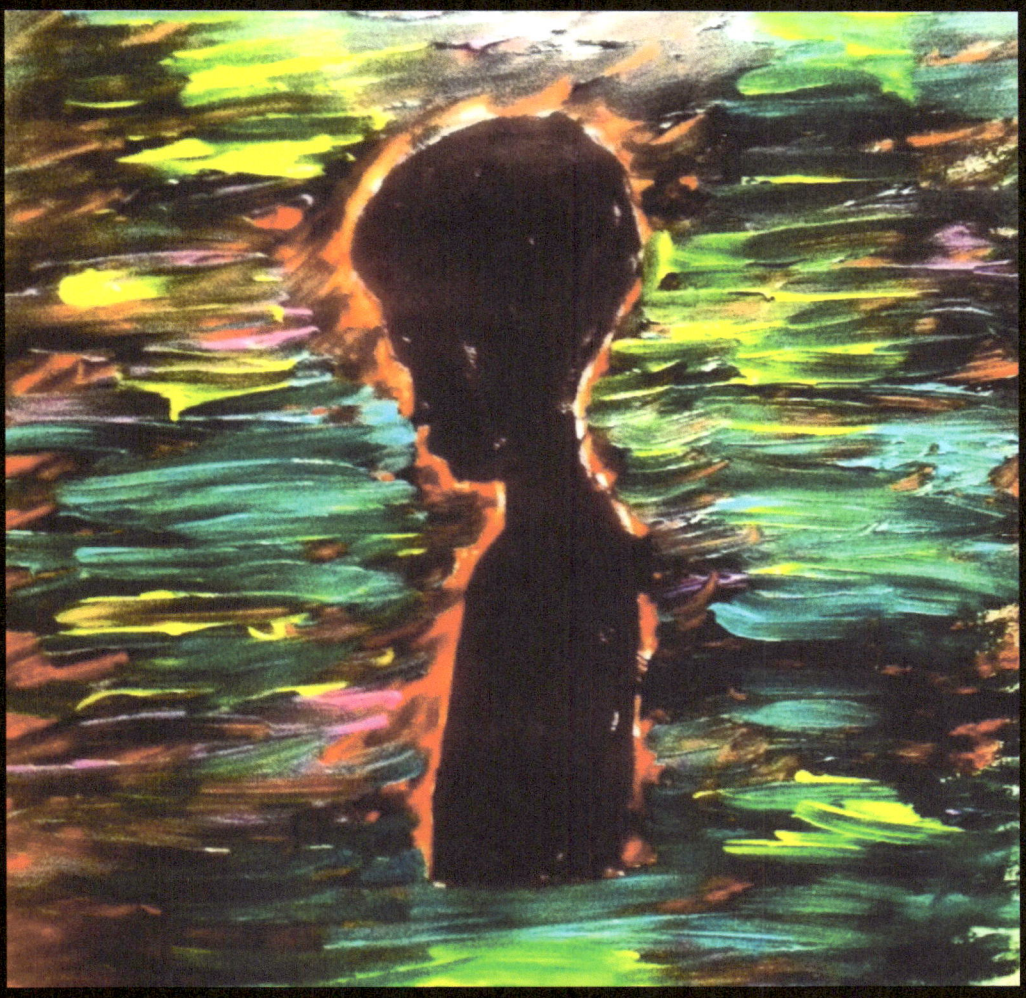

Acrylic paint on Canson, Mix-Media paper. 18 in x 24 in.

Detroit, Michigan 2015.

Bond

Our bond is forever

we should never lose touch.

The love we share is infinite

disagreements are obstacles,

not conclusions.

The devil is an illusion.

We create our reality.

You reside in my heart

even though we are a part.

I pray for clarity

but the disparity

between us

got mama losing sleep.

No smiles around the holidays.

Time is flying.

The distant keeps my soul crying.

We gotta do better.

Break the cycle

end the curse

because our relationship

Is worth fighting for.

Queen of ALL

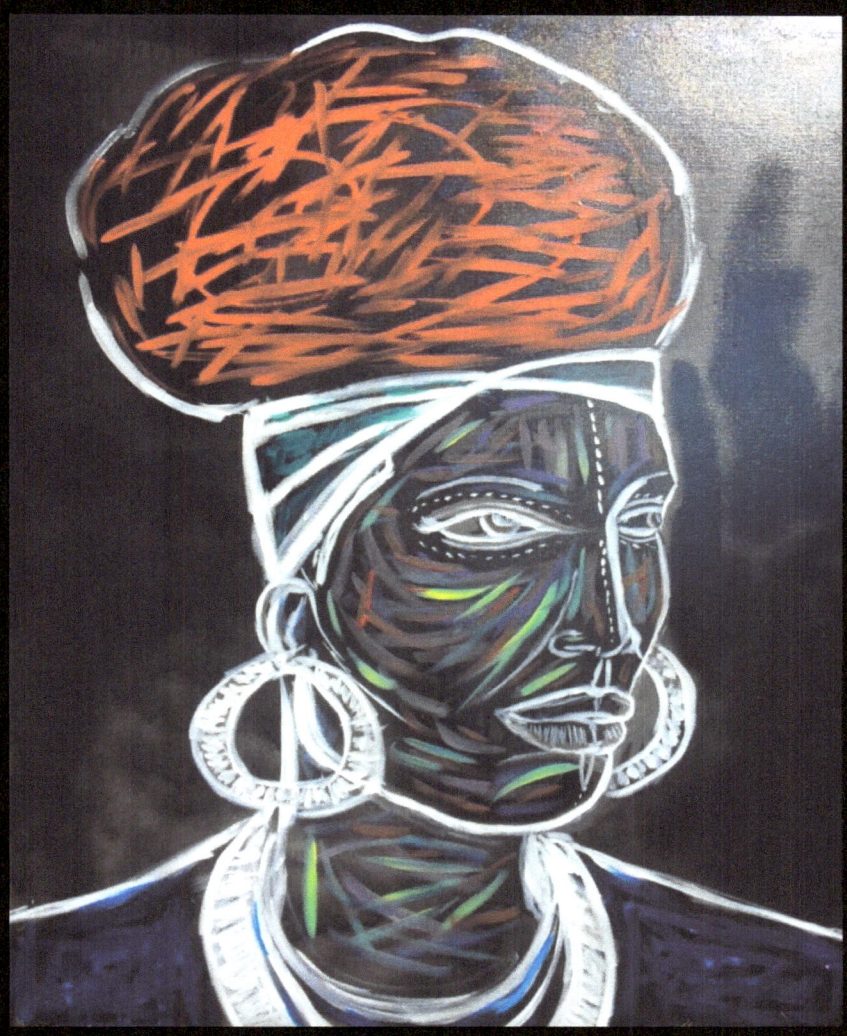

Acrylic painting on canvas. 36 in x 48 in.

Redford, Michigan 2017.

Fly Queen, Fly.

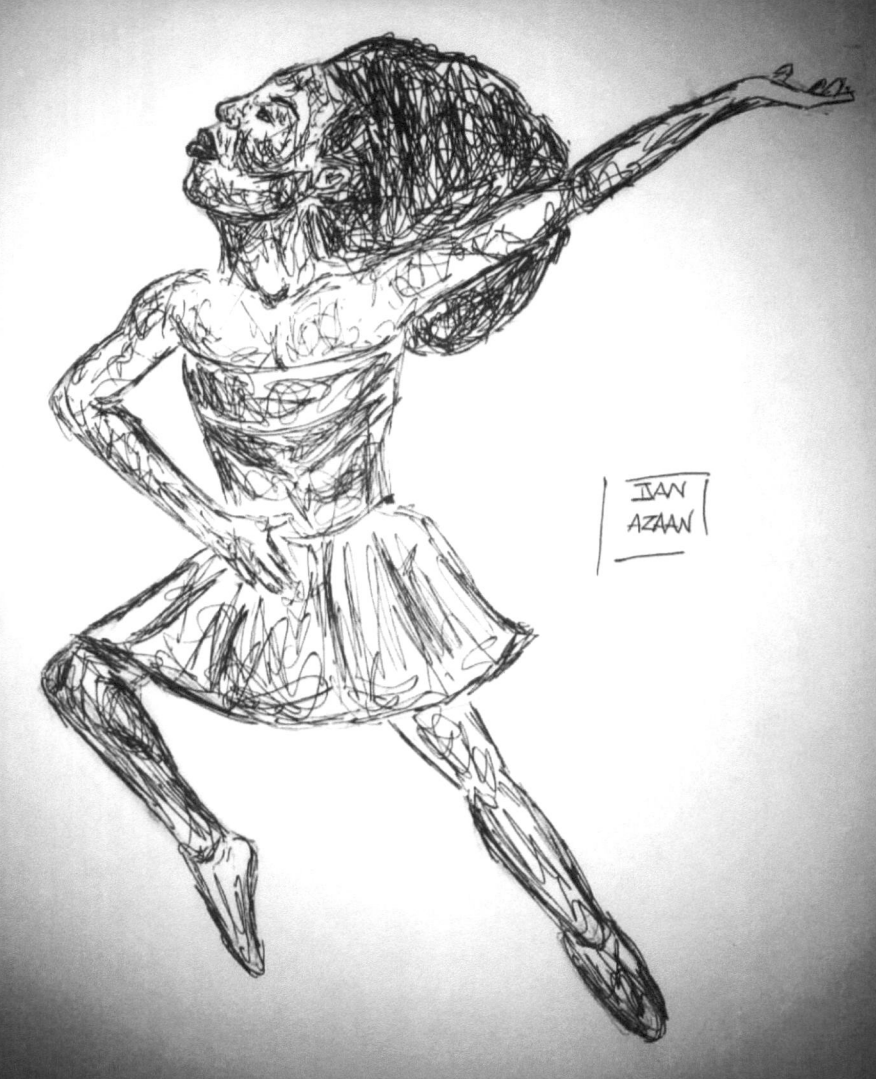

Pen drawing on Canson, Mix-Media paper. 18 in x 24 in.

Redford, Michigan 2017.

The Dancer

She moves

Flawlessly

Becomes one with the elements.

Every step

Is effortless.

She is unstoppable.

Her and the music

become synonymous.

With each word

Each drum

Each piano key

She becomes free

This is her release.

FLawless

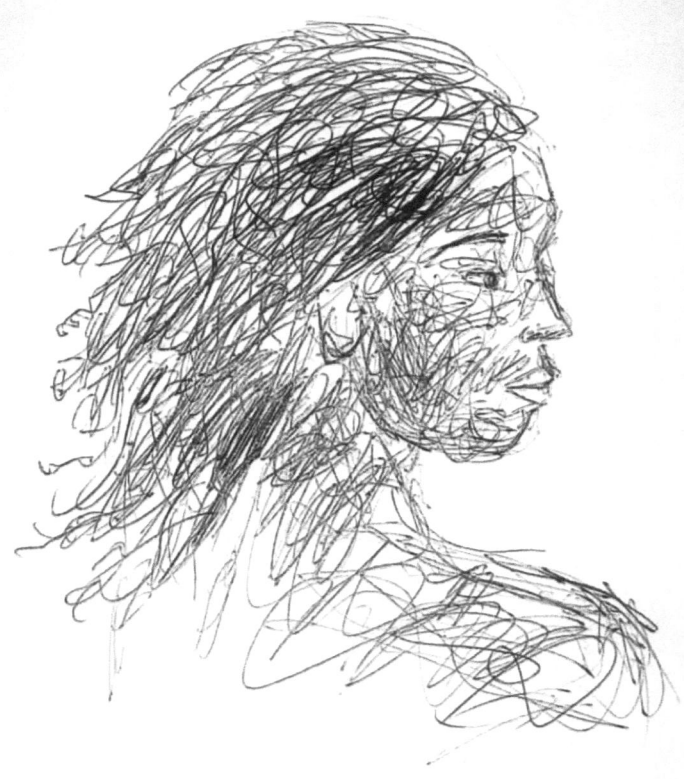

Pen drawing on Canson, Mix-Media paper. 18 in x 24 in.

Strong Woman

The beauty of her is unpredictable

As the layers of her unfold

Her story is told

The ink from each page of her life

Reveals all her insecurities

Dripping and drenched in her essence

I started to learn

The reason behind her strong exterior

Not inferior

Just in fear of

Disappointment.

Submerged

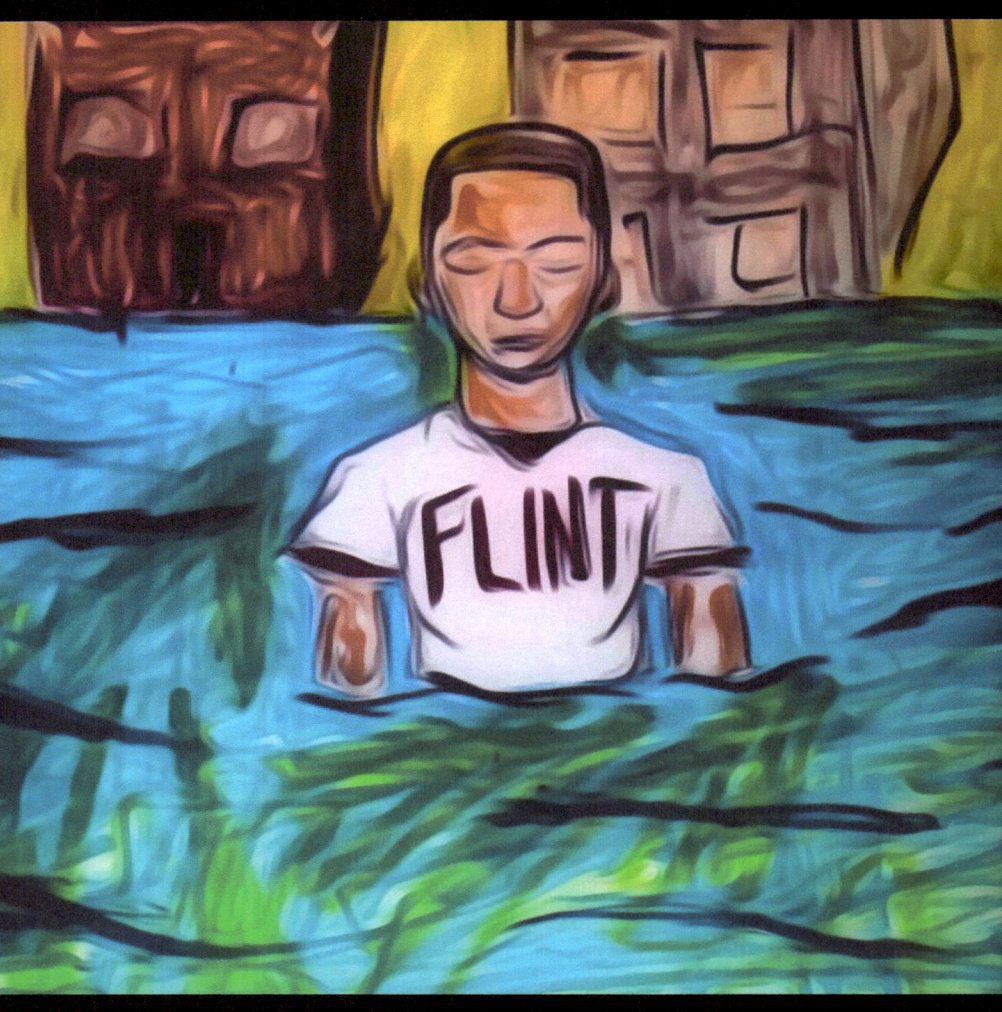

Digital Art

Flint

Dirty water

Cold streets

Financial struggles

They knew.

You were dying

Crying for hope

While drinking pollution.

They knew.

Suffering for years

Lack of education

No resources

They knew.

High death rates

Poverty

Abandoned houses

They knew.

You laid in those streets

Dying

Begging for help

They knew.

They knew

For a long time

And they did nothing.

Bullets Ain't Got No Name

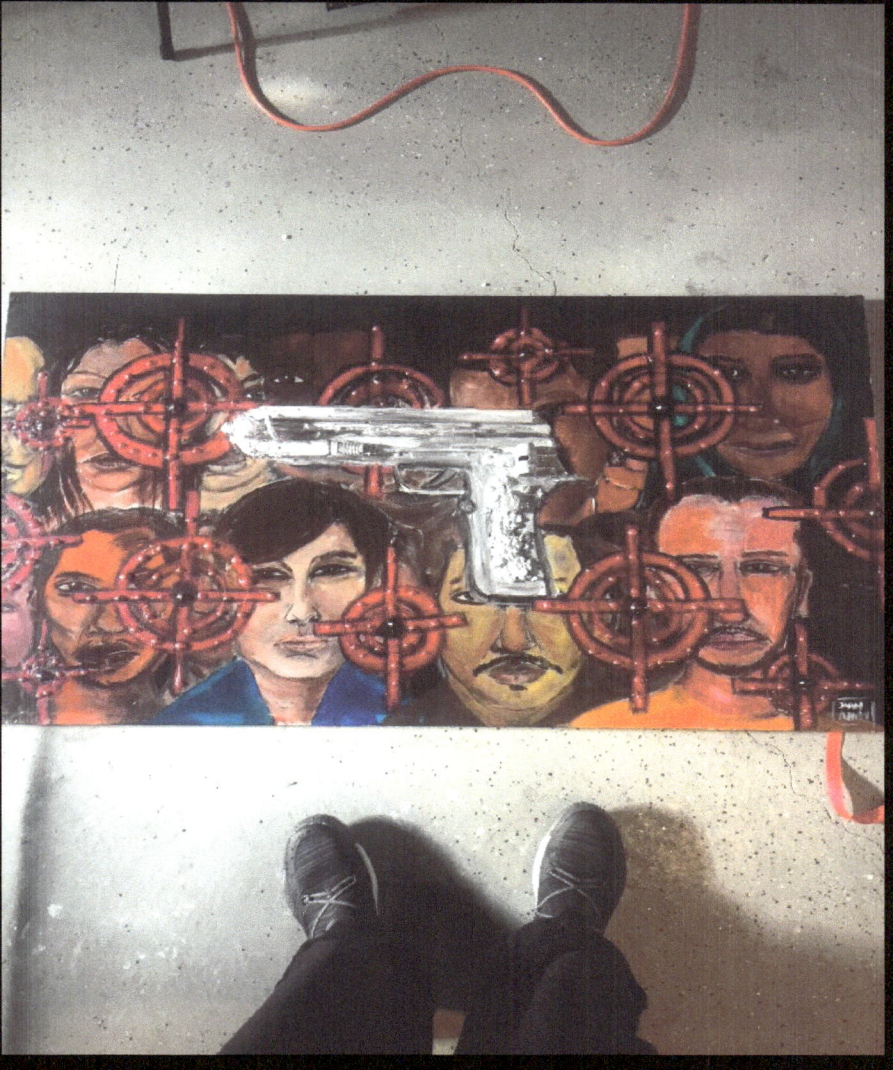

Mixed Media painting on wood.

Redford, Michigan 2017.

For Sandra

Black

Beautiful

And strong

You were all of that

The way you died

You didn't deserve that

Stuck in the cell

I refuse to believe you did that.

Power

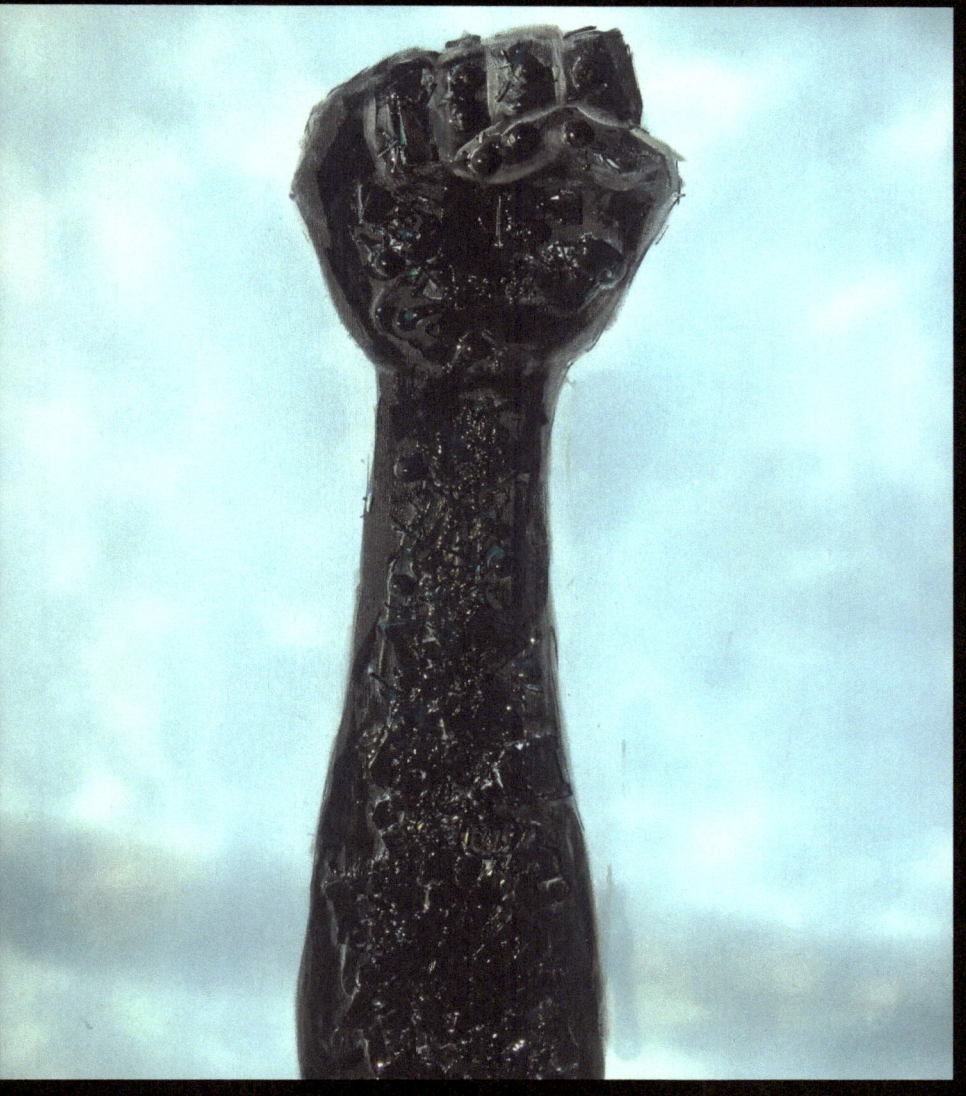

Mixed Media painting on canvas. 18 in x 24 in.

Redford, Michigan 2017.

Release

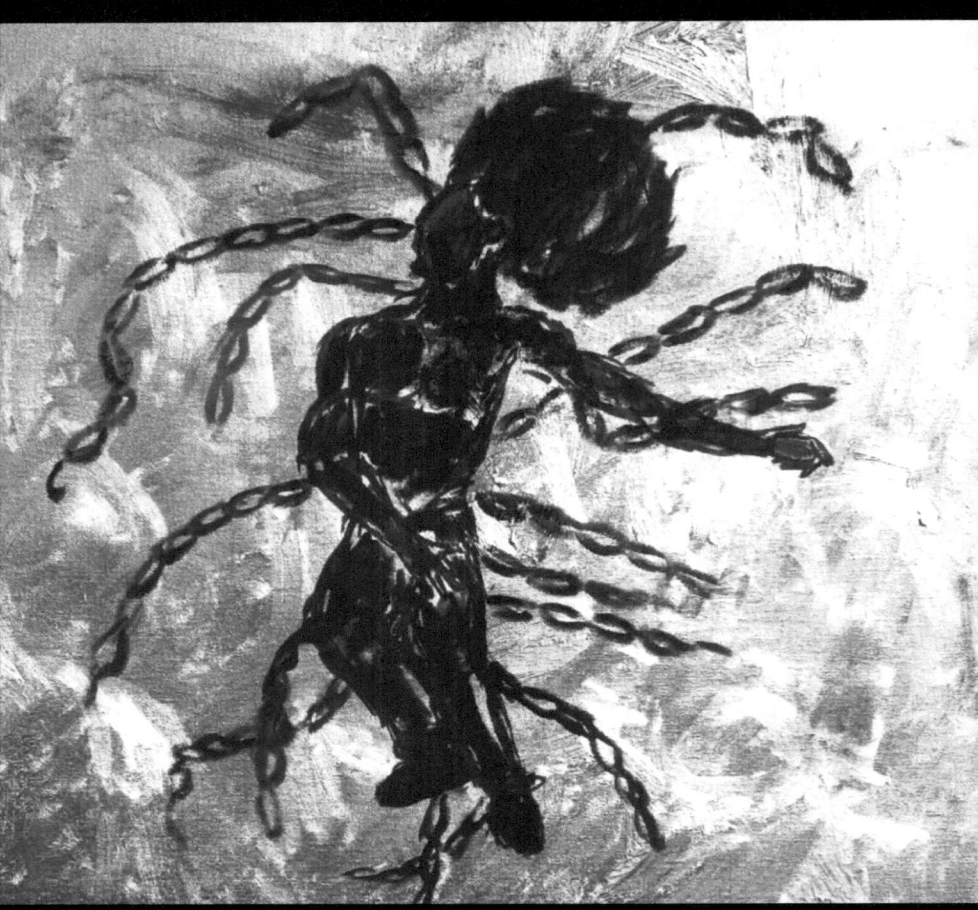

Mixed Media painting on canvas. 16 in X 20 in.

Trayvon

Young brother

You didn't die in vain

Your memory

Resonates.

In the midst of hate

we stand together

because of you.

We fight because of you

Because of you

Black lives matter.

Culture

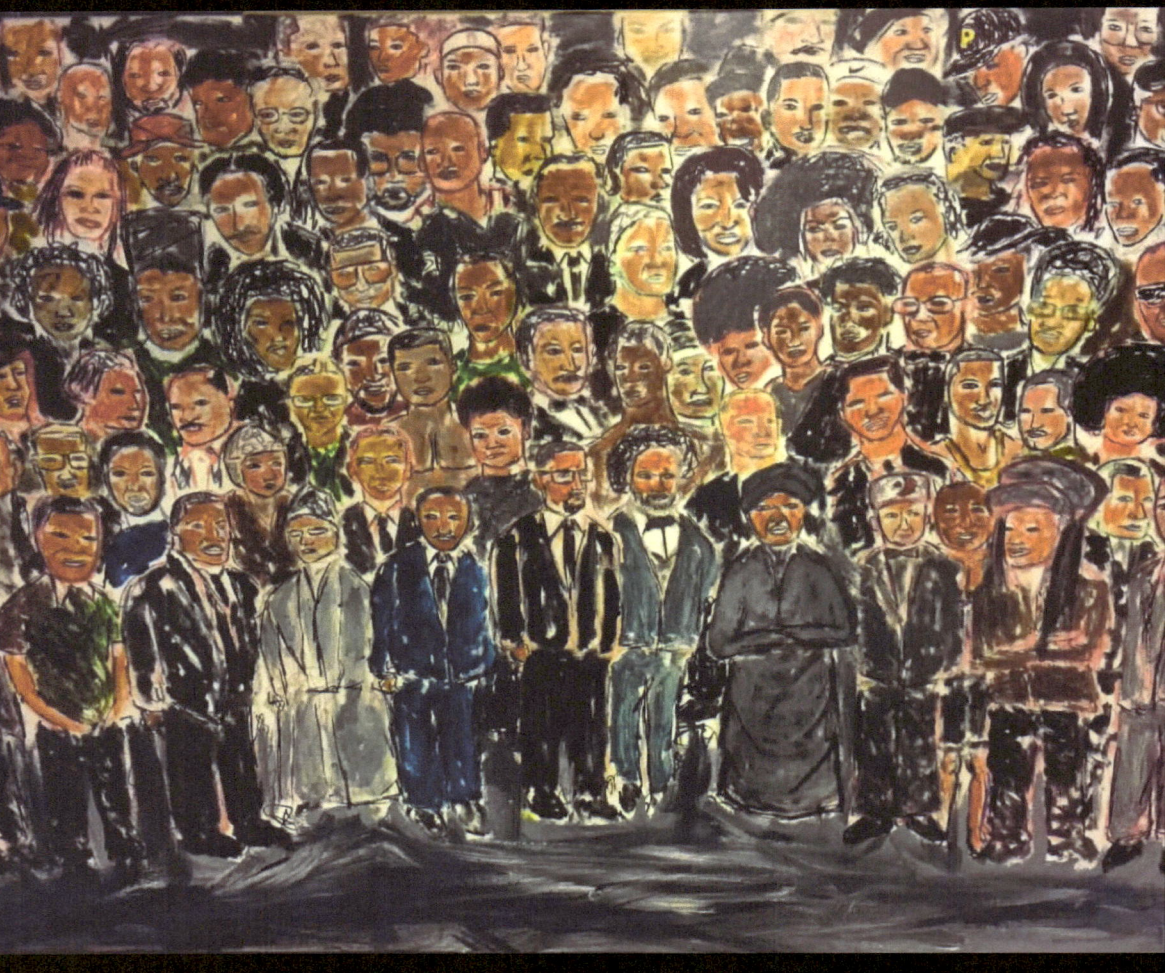

Acrylic painting on canvas. 18 in x 24 in.

Southfield, Michigan 2015.

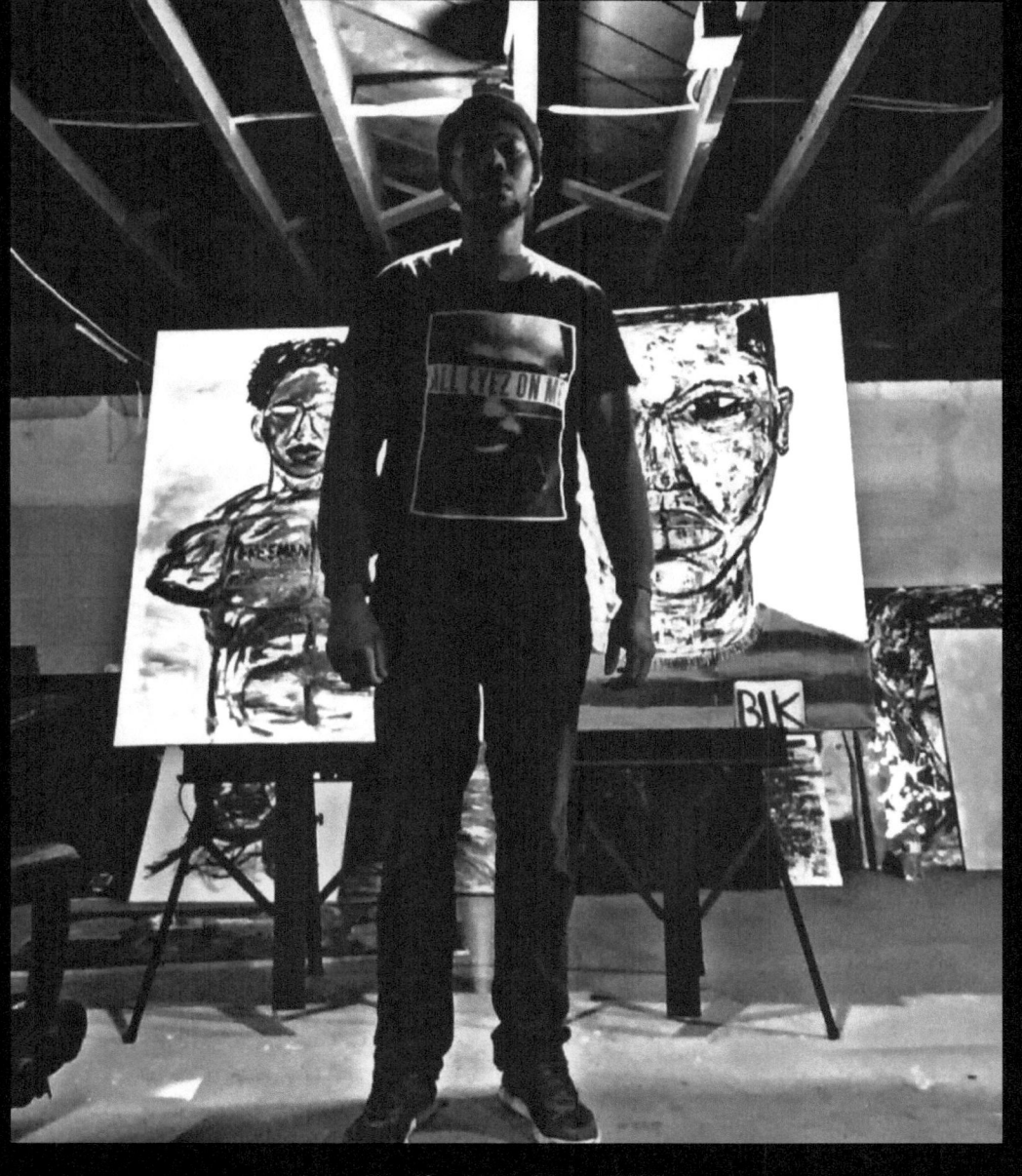

Redford, Michigan 2017.

Targets

Blood stained concrete

6 feet underneath

Dark days become your future

Because of a scared shooter

In fear of your complexion

For people of color

There is no protection

no help

from a country in denial

We are rivals!

They are killing our babies

Stealing our sons

But they tell you we are all ONE

I don't believe the dream

King would frown

Langston would talk about dreams being deferred

And the people would say

They simply want to be heard

Voiceless

Mute

Their only response is to shoot

Killing fathers

Brothers and sons

For them

the sun will shine no more

Only on their graves

Highlight their names

And death days

It seems like

We are targets

They use us as shooting practice

Putting bullets in innocent black bodies

Seems like a hobby for those who lobby for less gun control.

African American TEARS

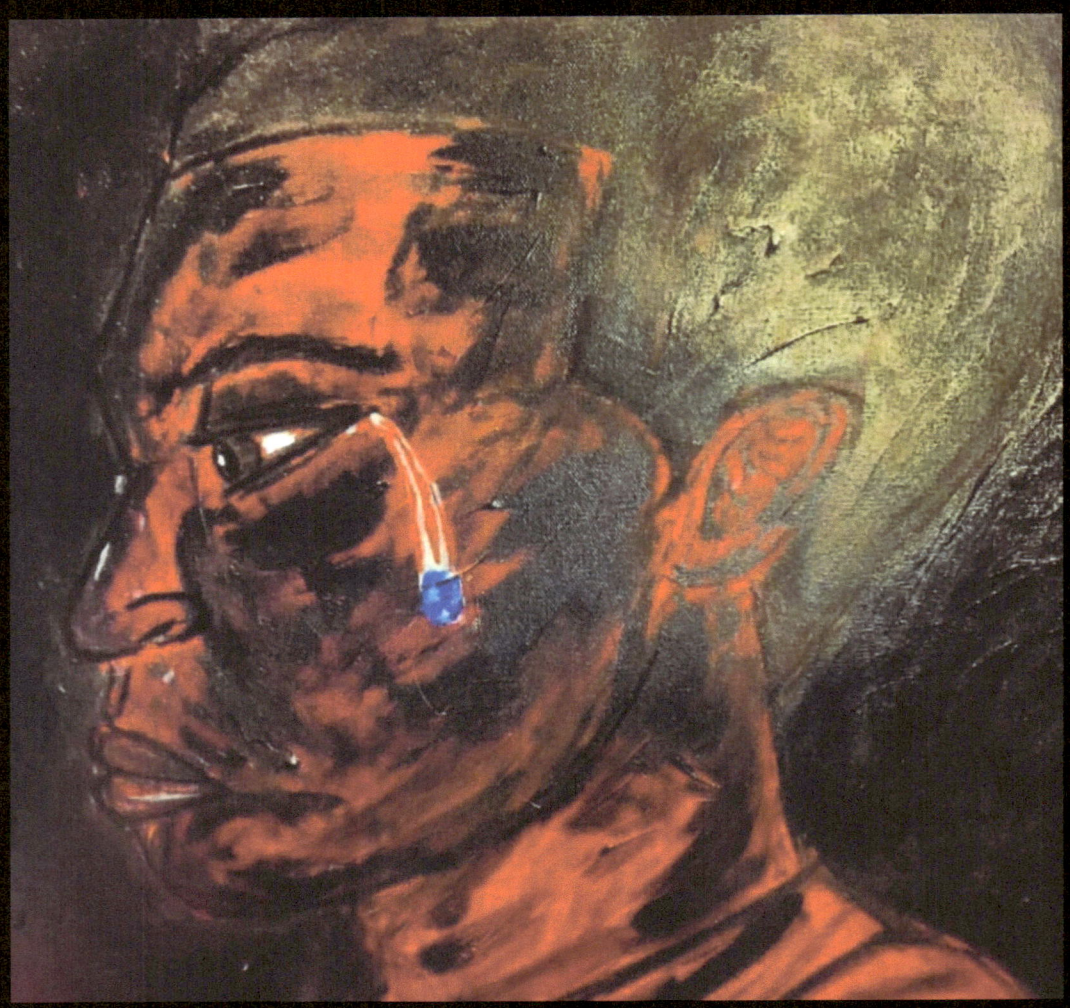

Acrylic painting on canvas. 16 in X 20 in.

Redford, Michigan 2017.

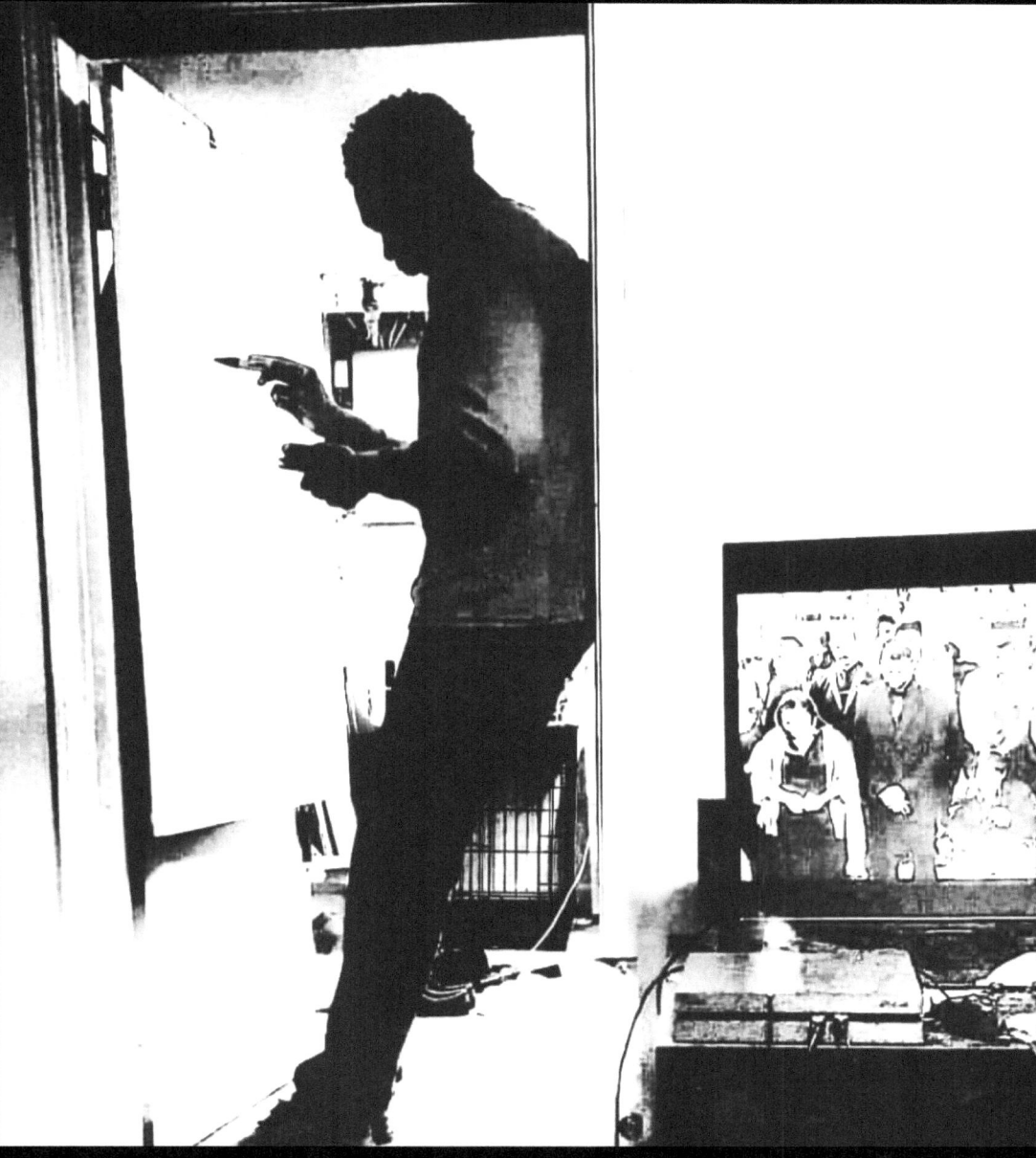

Detroit, Michigan 2015.

Puerto Rico

Irma left you

with

No power

Countless hours of darkness

No clarity

No help

Forgotten

Lost in foreign territory

But you call it home

Exposed lines

Exposed lies

For you I pray

and hope the world hears the voices that say

We need you!

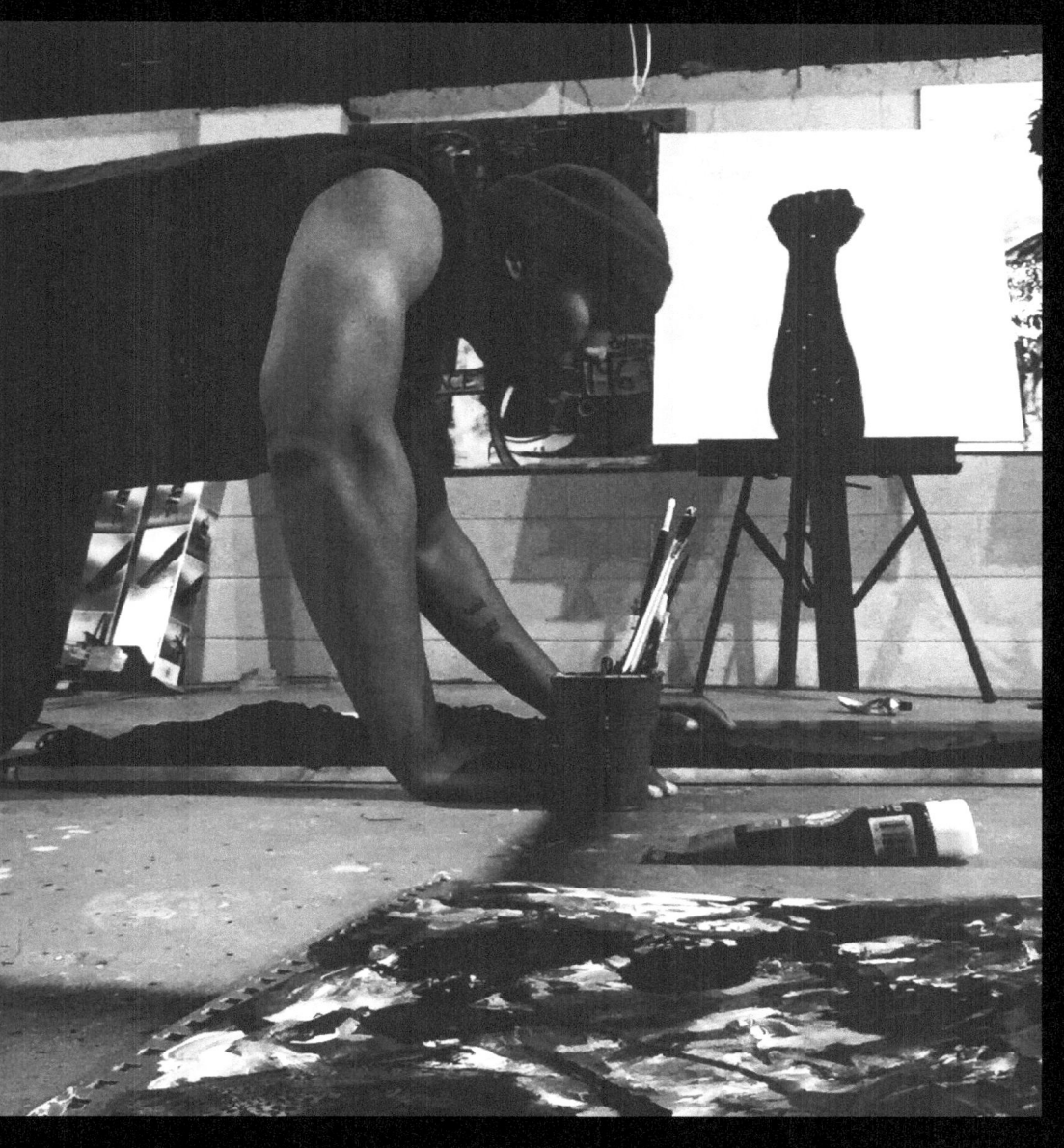

Redford, Michigan 2017

Revolt

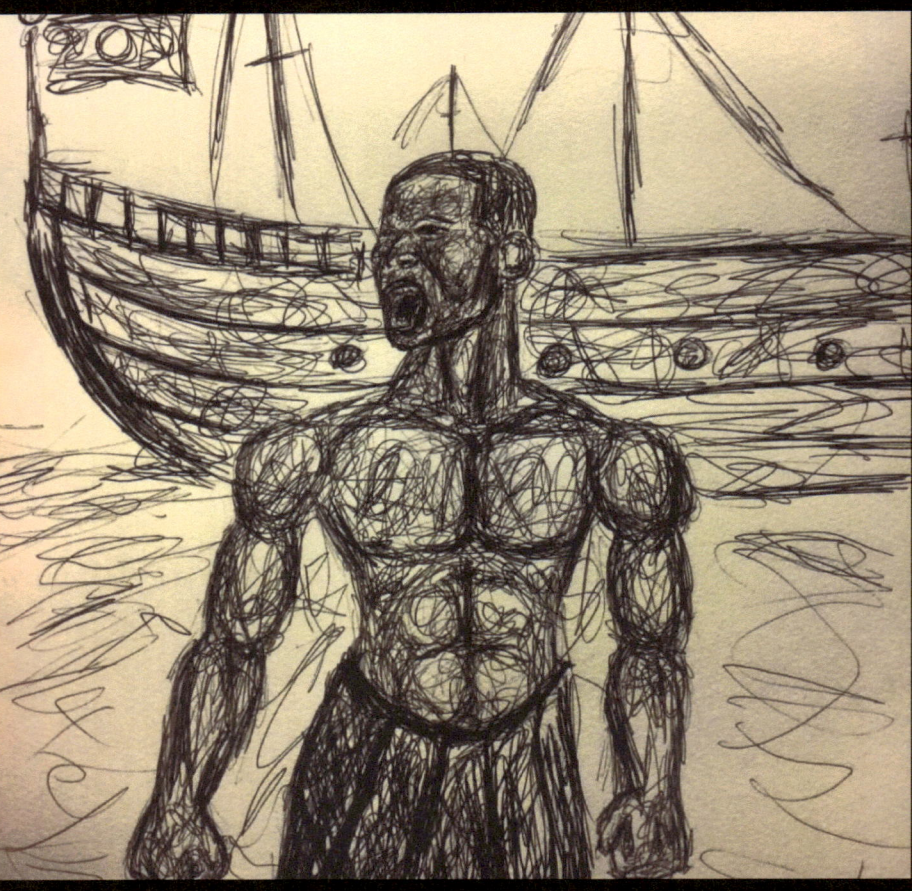

Pen drawing on Canson, Mix-Media paper. 11 in x 14 in.

Redford, Michigan 2017.

Gift + Curse

Born out of sequence

No symmetry could define me

disfigured

young figure

I was out of shape

Running on that treadmill

Chasing a meal

I suffered from malnutrition

born stigmatized

they criticize

because

I couldn't maintain a proper diet.

My family is a product of the riots

Stories of Rodney King's

and Emmet Till's

Unreported

and only one motive

Hopeless

and they know this

I hope they notice

We have been evicted

homeless

since the beginning

no privilege

we stay lifted though

Trying to get close to the gods

And find peace

It's a war out there

And the world is so unparalleled

We keep searching for equality

In a system focused on sovereignty

Third World dreams

But, really

It's a nightmare

They ain't got no food or water

But do we really care

Out of sight out of mind

We stay confined

And our favorite thing to say is "Next time"

Or maybe tomorrow

But by then it might be too late

We are in dire need

We got football players taking knees

Black boys taking bullets

If you ask me

It's all a bunch of bullshit

It's cool to stay lit

But it's also cool to stay woke

Aware

Conscious

This is higher learning

No John Singleton

But many men wish death

Upon me

Literally

Taking shots

More than 50

Diallo

Decomposing souls

Tell a drunken story

Hard times

Keep us reflecting

Thinking about history

And all the damage caused

I'm asking God to bulletproof these walls

because this life matters

and I need protection

A spiritual weapon

Mama pray for your sun

because every day is a battle

I refuse to settle

because you taught me better

So I'm out here working

Working like John Henry

But ain't no robot gon' beat me

They will not defeat me

I feel God in me

Running through my veins

He keeps me sane

When I'm swimming in pain

I keep my head to the sky

I promise you

I will leave my mark on this Earth

Before I die.

Natural Beauty

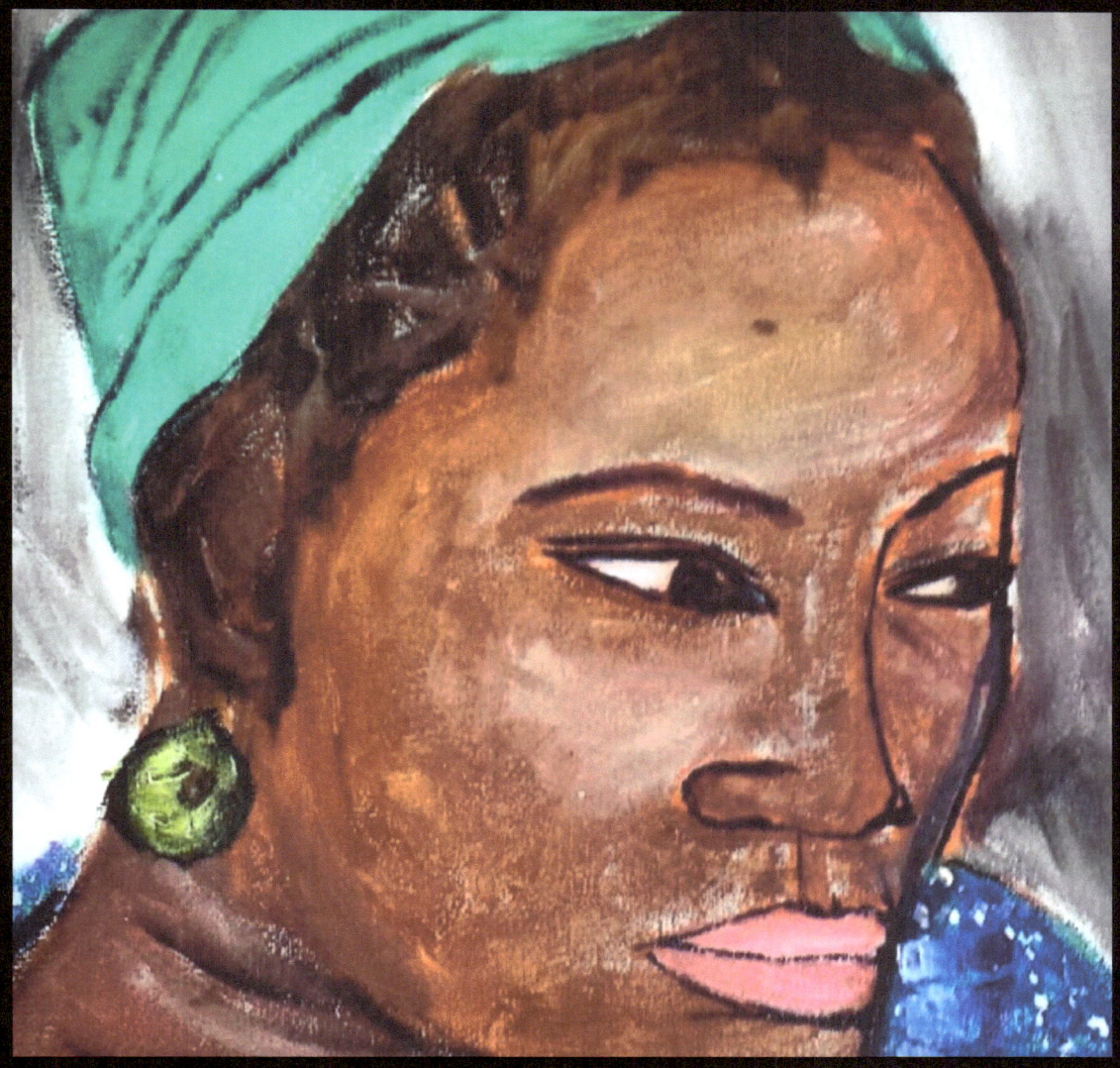

Acrylic painting on canvas. 16 in X 20 in.

Romulus, Michigan 2016.

The Vow

I see God in You

Your scriptures give me peace

Resurrect my universe

and make me understand my worth

With every verse you speak

I find love

You are my Genesis

and my Revelation

Without you

There's no me

Through you

I see a better me

and those lonely nights

Talking to my pillow

Are no more

You are my wife

My friend

my lover

And I know one day you will make the best mother

I guess what I'm trying to say

Is

I love you

Forever...

Together

we are one

never separated.

Lord knows

this is why we were created.

Today I promise you

I will give my all

Be strong when you are weak

Be that ear when you're ready to speak.

You are my queen

I can't wait to spend my life with you

and cherish every moment.

I look forward to

laughing until our stomachs hurt

Listening to music until the sun rises

Talking until our voices become hoarse

I look forward to it all

As long as all of it

Is with you.

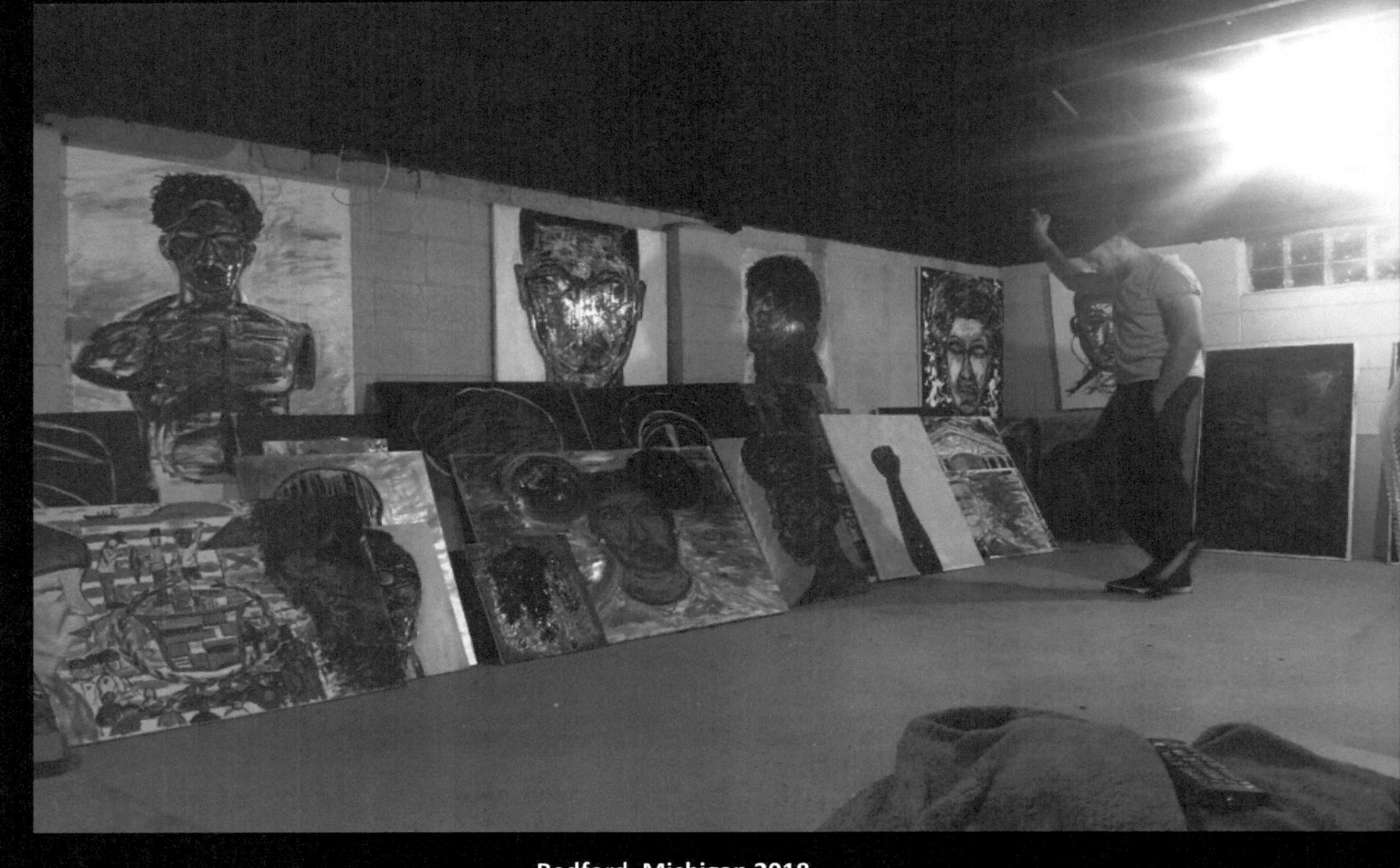

Redford, Michigan 2018.

www.ingramcontent.com/pod-product-compliance
Lightning Source LLC
Chambersburg PA
CBHW040741200526
45159CB00023B/1124